£2.49

(P)

PETER GUTTRIDGE

The Great
Train Robbery

———

the national archives

First published in 2008 by
The National Archives
Kew, Richmond
Surrey, TW9 4DU, UK
www.nationalarchives.gov.uk

The National Archives
brings together the Public Record Office,
Historical Manuscripts Commission,
Office of Public Sector Information
and Her Majesty's Stationery Office.

A catalogue card for this book is available from the British Library.

ISBN 978 1 905615 32 2

Cover illustrations: Bruce Reynolds (Getty Images);
Ronnie Biggs (TNA FCO 53/400); Buster Edwards (Getty Images);
the Glasgow–London mail train (Getty Images).
Jacket design and typesetting by Goldust Design
Page design by Ken Wilson | point 918
Picture research by Gwen Campbell
Printed in Great Britain by
The Cromwell Press Ltd, Trowbridge, Wiltshire

Contents

—

Heist of the Century

The Great Train Robbery of 1963 remains one of the most audacious crimes of the twentieth century—and the most profitable. The £2.6 million (worth around £50 million in 2008) taken early in the morning of Thursday 8 August from the Glasgow to London night mail train was the largest amount of cash ever stolen in Britain until the 2006 Securitas depot raid in which £53 million was taken.

To be sure there have been other bigger hauls, but not of cash. In 1990 a petty thief mugged a financial messenger in the City of London and relieved him of £292 million worth of bonds. In 1983, 20 years after the Great Train Robbery, six men poured petrol over a security guard at the Brinks-Mat high-security vault at Heathrow Airport and threatened to burn him alive if he did not open the vault. They got away with £26 million in gold bullion and diamonds.

But bonds, bullion and diamonds are hard to shift and lose their value in the process. The City of London mugger was murdered between arrest and trial, presumably by those he had contacted to try to sell on the bonds. All but two of the bearer bonds were recovered. Little of the Brinks-Mat loot has ever been traced, but it would have needed melting down and disposing of in some different form. Some £21 million of the Securitas money has been recovered.

By contrast, the vast quantity of used £5 and £1 notes stolen on that balmy summer night in 1963 at the rail signal at Sears Crossing were, mostly, untraceable — and, indeed, less than one seventh of the money was ever recovered.

The robbers, too, would have been untraceable had they not spoiled the efficient execution of their remarkably simple plan by making stupid blunders after they had committed an almost perfect crime.

The biggest train robbery in history was quickly dubbed the crime of the century. Although the British press did not condone the robbery — especially as the train driver, Jack Mills, had been brutally coshed into submission — in America there was admiration. After all, the US had produced Jesse James (hitherto the most famous train robber) and the silent film that gave this crime its name.

The *New York Times* commented: 'How pallid our own crime syndicates are made to look, how wanting in imagination.' Whilst acknowledging the US's role as 'a cultural inspiration', the newspaper noted: 'the know-how is distinctly British' (quoted in Anthony Delano's *Slip-up: How Fleet Street Caught Ronnie Biggs and Scotland Yard Lost Him*). Another New York paper, the *Herald Tribune*, had a front-page headline that read: 'History's Greatest Robbery — There'll Always Be An England'. Inside, the newspaper commented on 'the exceptional finesse' with which 'British criminals do their work' (Delano).

As the sixties advanced, the Great Train Robbers took their place in western popular culture alongside those other British world-beaters, the Beatles and James Bond.

The year 1963 was one of transition. 'Mopheads' replaced Brylcreemed quiffs as the hairstyle of choice when the Beatles and the Liverpool Sound took the Hit Parade away from Cliff Richard, The Shadows and the teddy boys. (President John F. Kennedy had already unsettled an older generation by going hat-less, plunging the US hat industry into irreversible decline.) And according to Philip Larkin in his poem 'Annus Mirabilis', it was the year in which sex was invented — though the ban on *Lady Chatterley* referred to in his poem was actually lifted in 1960.

Larkin might have been referring in part to the Profumo scandal. In March 1963 the then Secretary of State for War, John Profumo, lied to the Commons about his brief affair with a good-time girl called Christine Keeler, whom he had met at a party at Cliveden, the historic stately home. By the early summer he had admitted lying and resigned.

The establishment looked for someone to punish. Keeler was imprisoned and Stephen Ward, the man who had introduced her to Profumo, was prosecuted for living off immoral earnings. He killed himself on the last day of the trial.

The impact of the scandal caused massive damage to the Tory government. Prime Minister Harold Macmillan resigned in October 1963, claiming poor health, and a year later Labour came to power.

There was a spying angle to the Profumo affair as Keeler had also been involved with a Russian military attaché. But then spies seemed to be everywhere in 1963, in fiction and in fact, as the Cold War cast a dark shadow over the world. The previous year had seen the establishment of the Berlin Wall and the narrow avoidance of nuclear war during the Cuban Missile Crisis. William Vasill had been given an 18-year gaol sentence for spying for Russia after being caught in a KGB homosexual honey-trap. 1963 pretty much began with the announcement that Kim Philby was the 'third man' in the Burgess–Maclean spy scandal.

In fiction, some writers were reflecting the drab reality of spies, pre-eminently Len Deighton in *The Ipcress File* (1962) and John Le Carré in *The Spy Who Came In From The Cold* (1963). However, the most famous spy in the world — Ian Fleming's James Bond — was much more glamorous, especially on celluloid, played by Sean Connery in *Dr No* (1962).

The popularity of such glossy escapism reflected in Britain the beginning of a move from the austerity of the fusty fifties to the relative plenty of the swinging sixties. For working-class youth, a career in pop music was one way to share the sixties affluence. Crime was another.

The Great Train Robbers were by now a generation or so too old to be pop stars, but most of them had criminal records going back to their own teens in the late forties. And they were all working class, primarily from the poor areas of south London. They were a mix of chancers, petty crooks, more ambitious thieves and hard men. Many had worked together in some configuration or other before, and most had done time in prison. Together they pulled off what at first appeared to be the perfect crime. However, it quickly fell apart. By January 1964 there were 12 men on trial with three others identified but on the run. Then reality exceeded fiction as not one but two of those convicted made spectacular prison breaks and also went on the run.

One of these—Ronnie Biggs—became the best-known robber simply because he remained free until he gave himself up in 2001. In fact, he was a painter and decorator and some-time petty crook who was only a minor member of the gang. Buster Edwards, a more senior member, found fame in 1988 with the release of the film *Buster* in which he was played as a cockney cheeky chappie by rock star Phil Collins with national treasure Julie Walters as his wife.

However, the most interesting and probably most important of the robbers were Charlie Wilson (the other escapee) and two of the men who immediately went on the run: Bruce Reynolds and Jimmy White. Then there's Gordon Goody, a man who was certainly guilty, but who was quite possibly 'fitted up' by the police in order to produce a conviction.

In 1963 the public's view of the police was largely formed by watching the avuncular *Dixon of Dock Green* on television. Even the arrival of the grittier, Liverpool-set *Z Cars* the previous year did nothing to shake the public's faith in the incorruptibility of the police. However, we now know that some members of the London-based Flying Squad and police in other divisions of the country's police forces were corrupt. Between 1972 and 1976 some 82 Metropolitan Police officers were dismissed and 301 left voluntarily in the middle of disciplinary or criminal enquiries. A further 46 were suspended. A number of these officers would have been serving in 1963 (Barry Cox, John Shirley and Martin Short's *The Fall of Scotland Yard*).

A CRIMINAL MASTERMIND?

In fiction a crime as well executed as the Great Train Robbery would never have been pulled off by a bunch of working-class villains without some criminal mastermind, probably from a different class, to organize it and thereafter pull their strings. The title of the popular 1960 British film *League of Gentlemen*, about a bank heist executed by ex-servicemen, was ironic but nevertheless the ingenious robbery was planned by a retired lieutenant colonel (played with weary urbanity by Jack Hawkins) with help from ex-commissioned officers. The working-class 'other ranks' were on hand only to do the hard graft.

There was much talk in the press at the time of the Great Train Robbery of a criminal mastermind behind the plot. The *Sunday Telegraph* on the first weekend after the heist wrote of 'a miser who lives alone in one room in Brighton'. This man 'works with infinite care and patience' to come up with criminal plans he then takes to 'a master criminal well known in the Harrow Road area of London'.

This seems unlikely, but the concept of a shadowy evil genius proved contagious. Journalist Peta Fordham, wife of one of the barristers involved in the defence of the robbers, wrote the first book about the robbers and the robbery in 1965. I find *The Robbers' Tale* difficult to read today because of sentences like: 'As the late G.K. Chesterton once remarked to my father-in-law'. However, in it she claims knowledge that there was a criminal brain behind the robbery.

For her this mastermind wasn't a miser in Brighton but a man of intelligence, an 'uncrowned intellectual king of the underworld'. This man came up with the plan of robbing a mail train, but then got bored with it. The plan, however, 'was floating about the underworld' for years, a master job just waiting for someone with the nerve to attempt it.

Fordham explained that she didn't know the 'present' name of this Moriarty figure — but claimed that, if pressed, she could name him.

She never did so, however.

A decade or so later a South African literary agent, Gary

van Dyk, went to publishers W.H. Allen and offered the full story of the robbery from the point of view of seven of the robbers who had just been released on parole, with the approval of two who were still in gaol and Ronnie Biggs who was in Brazil. The distinguished author Piers Paul Read was invited to write their account (*The Train Robbers: Their Story*). In it the robbers claimed not so much that there was a mastermind behind the crime as that they had a financier, a German who put up £80,000 to plan and carry out the robbery in return for £1 million of the take. He was identified as none other than Otto Skorzeny, the Waffen-SS commander who during the Second World War had carried out the spectacular rescue of Mussolini from Gran Sasso.

In Read's account one of Skorzeny's men — 'Sigi' — was at Leatherslade Farm; more of his men broke Charlie Wilson out of prison; and yet others spirited Buster Edwards out of the country and arranged for plastic surgery for him. Read believes all this in the introduction to his entertaining book, but by chapter 13 recognizes that the robbers have conned him in order to make their story more saleable.

Almost equally entertaining is the wholly unfounded but persistent rumour that motor racing mogul Bernie Ecclestone was the brains behind the Great Train Robbery. In an interview for the *Independent* in April 2005 he was asked outright if he masterminded the robbery. He jokingly responded: 'There wasn't enough money on that train. I could have done something better than that.' He went on to explain that the rumour came from the fact that a racing driver, Roy James, was the getaway driver. (In fact, although James was indeed a getaway driver and was one of the robbers, there was no getaway car at the robbery.) When James came out of prison he asked Eccle-stone for a job. 'I owned Brabham at the time [James's choice of racing car], but I wasn't going to let him drive for me.' Instead James, a skilled silversmith, was invited to make a trophy for Ecclestone.

A MURKY AFFAIR

The stories of a mastermind point to one of the frustrating things about researching the Great Train Robbery. Nobody but the robbers on the track that August night knows for sure what happened.

The National Archives has a vast amount of information about the robbery from court transcripts and police files. But as most of the robbers pleaded not guilty, their statements are not accurate accounts of what happened. Those who pleaded guilty were equally unforthcoming. The police files give little inside information since the investigators didn't really have any.

Whilst there is ample evidence from the events surrounding the Great Train Robbery that there is little honour among thieves, where these particular thieves are concerned they have continued to show a loyalty to each other that means a number of questions about the robbery remain unanswered or have been answered with lies.

For instance, it is probable there were at least two other men on the track who got away scot-free. There is nothing in the National Archives about this. In the 45 years since the robbery not a single one of the known robbers has said who those men were.

The beating driver Jack Mills received to subdue him prevents the Great Train Robbery being seen as a larky heist. Yet the identity of the man who coshed him remains a mystery. Buster Edwards said that he did it in Piers Paul Read's book, but 20 years later Bruce Reynolds says in his *The Autobiography of A Thief* that it was one of the men who got away. According to Reynolds, Edwards confessed because part of the deal with the publisher was that the identity of the man who hit Mills be revealed.

Reynolds' autobiography is a major secondary source, but is to be taken with a pinch of salt, partly because, like most of us, he is self-aggrandizing and partly because he has a markedly romantic — indeed cinematic — view of events.

The two books based on conversations with the robbers — those of Peta Fordham and Piers Paul Read — also need to be handled with care, although Fordham claims an inside knowledge. Read admits he was hoodwinked, which makes his book suspect as an accurate record.

Going by the evidence in the National Archives, police memoirs are equally suspect since there is no indication that the police had any idea of who did what. The judge in the first trial famously stated that since it was impossible to work out who had done what either in the planning or execution of the crime he was going to give most of the accused exactly the same sentence: 30 years.

CHAPTER ONE

At Sears Crossing

When the glass shattered — ugly, jagged shards crashing to the floor — and the hulking masked man with the broad-bladed axe in his hands pitched through the window, the five postal workers knew it was over. The heavy mailbags they had been desperately piling against the door were tumbling down as more men, armed with pickaxe handles and coshes, in boiler suits and woollen masks, pushed into the carriage.

The postal workers were brave, but their job was sorting mail, not fighting off ruthless men, one of whom they thought they had heard moments before shout from the track: 'They're bolting the door — get the guns.'

It was around 3.15 am on a clear warm night at Sears Crossing in Buckinghamshire. The postal workers were all in the High Value Package (HVP) carriage of the night mail train, which had left Glasgow at 6.05 pm. Three of them — Thomas Kett, Frank Dewhurst and Leslie Penn — had been in this carriage since the train started its journey. The other two — Joseph Ware and John O'Connor — had joined the train at Tamworth and had only been sent down to this carriage a few minutes before the train had ground to a halt at Sears Crossing.

Until it had stopped, the rattle of the train over the points and the steady clack–clack rhythm had counter pointed the tempo of the work. Even when the train halted the postal workers didn't really pay much attention. Such temporary stops were a common occurrence on the long nightly journey as there had been electrification work going on for months.

A few minutes later the train had shunted forward. Then stopped again. None of them had thought anything of it — until, that is, a gang of men had tried to force their way into the carriage and then the big man crashed through the window.

Thomas Kett was an Assistant Inspector who was in charge of the train from Carlisle to London Euston. Frank Dewhurst, Postman Higher Grade, was in charge of this particular coach. Both men were hit with coshes and, along with their colleagues, forced to the floor of the carriage. Kett later stated that 'We were all hit with the various coshes. I myself was hit across the shoulder and the elbows' (J 82/420).

The postal workers must have been shocked. Travelling Post Offices had operated in Britain for 125 years and none had ever been robbed. The GPO's night sorting train had been made famous in *Night Mail*, a short promotional film from the 1930s that featured a poem by W.H. Auden. That particular train had been heading in the other direction. This train — the Glasgow to London travelling Post Office — was on its regular run. And this train was stuffed with money.

Banks outside London were required to hold sufficient money in their vaults for most eventualities, but any surplus was sent down to the head offices in the capital. At the start of its journey in Glasgow, this train took on board the surplus money from all Scottish banks in HVPs, loaded into one carriage. More HVPs were added at various stops en route to London. On this particular train, because there had just been a Scottish bank holiday, there was even more money than usual.

The HVP carriage was the second from the engine (see plate 2). In front of it was a parcels carriage. There was no corridor linking these two carriages. Behind the HVP were 10 more carriages containing 67 postal workers busy sorting ordinary mail to be distributed in London and the south later that morning. The HVPs were intended for East Central District Post Office for distribution to bank head offices.

The train was due to arrive at Euston at 4 am on Thursday morning. There were seven scheduled stops en route to pick up additional coaches. More bank money had also been loaded into the HVP carriage during the journey. It had been in sacks piled on the platforms at each station, guarded by police who virtually sequestered these stations until the money was loaded on the train. But on the train itself there was not a single policeman, transport policeman or security guard. No one was specifically responsible for guarding a massive amount of money. The later police report noted: 'There was no resistance by the GPO workers who were not expected to meet violence with violence. There was no real guard on nearly £3m' (HO 242/4).

As the postmen lay on the floor, more men crowded into the carriage. Two started stacking the mailbags stuffed with money and three others handed them down onto the railway line. There were 128 bags. The largest note was the fiver—both the big, older white version and the new blue one, half its size. The bags were also stuffed with pound notes and thousands of pounds worth of 10-shilling notes.

Within 25 minutes the robbers had stripped the carriage bare of all but seven of the bags. Then the driver and the fireman of the train were dragged into the carriage, handcuffed together, and dropped to the floor to lie beside the sorters. One of the robbers warned them: 'We're leaving someone behind —don't move for 30 minutes or it will be the worse for you.'

And then the robbers were gone.

THE DRIVER'S TALE

Just over 30 minutes earlier driver Jack Mills, age 58, had slowed the train at an amber light at Leighton Buzzard that gave warning that the next light might be red. 1,300 yards further on, at Sears Crossing, it was. He drew the train to a halt. It was 3.03 am.

He could see a light further down the line at green so suggested the 26-year-old fireman David Whitby (his title was fireman, but in reality he was the deputy driver) phone from the red signal to the signalman to ask what the problem was. Mills and Whitby had joined the train at Crewe. It had left there on time at 12.30 am and made scheduled stops at Tamworth and Rugby.

Whitby descended the 10 feet to the track and walked along to the signal. The phone was dead. He didn't know it then, but the wires had been cut.

As he came back towards the engine he saw a man walking towards him from between the second and third carriages on the other side of the tracks. He assumed he was either the signalman or someone from the train.

'What's up mate?' he called as the man waved for him to climb up the embankment.

He joined the man at the top of the embankment and the stranger immediately bundled him down the other side to where two other men, their faces concealed beneath balaclavas, grabbed him.

'Shout and we'll kill you,' one of them said, and Whitby saw something like a cosh in the man's hand.

'It's okay — I'm on your side,' Whitby said as they crowded round him.

'Where are you from?' one of the men said.

'Crewe,' Whitby replied, and the man promised they'd send him some money later.

In the cab of the train Mills, the driver, was waiting for Whitby's return. Instead of Whitby, however, a masked man tried to force his way up into the cab. What then happened is confused as testimonies disagree in some details, but the outcome is not in doubt.

Mills later stated that he suddenly became aware of a masked man climbing up the ladder into the cab, carrying an iron bar wrapped in a sack. He struggled with him in the confined space of the cab and felt he was succeeding in pushing the man off the train. Then another man came up behind Mills and hit him along the side of the head.

In his evidence in court, Mills's witness statement said: 'I was struck on the back of the head four times, twice on the side of the head and I was severely bruised upon the upper part of my body and head … They had all got staves in their hands and one had a piece of iron piping.'

The robbers had slightly different versions. The version they told their biographer, Piers Paul Read, was that one of the robbers was trying to climb the ladder up into the cab when Mills started kicking at his hands. Hanging on with one hand, the robber beat Mills about the legs with his cosh, but it was only when a robber grabbed Mills from behind that the driver lost the fight. According to this version, the first robber then climbed into the cab and, whilst Mills's arms were pinned to his side, hit the driver twice over the head. Blood started to pour down the driver's face and he fell to his knees. According to Peta Fordham the worst of Mills's injuries were caused by his banging his head as he dropped.

The severity of a head injury cannot be measured by the amount of blood that flows. The scalp has many blood vessels near the surface of the skin so that even minor wounds bleed excessively. One of the robbers wiped the blood from the driver's face with a rag and told him that he was not badly hurt.

Mills was dragged into the passageway behind the driver's compartment and handcuffed to Whitby. They were turned to face away from the front of the engine. They heard some tense words from inside the cab and then a robber came back to them. He grabbed Mills, taking the handcuffs off him and forcing him back in to the cab.

White-faced, bleeding and shaken, Mills was pushed down into his seat and ordered to move the train or he'd 'get some more'. Mills agreed, but it took a minute or two because the vacuum brake on the train was on and the pressure needed to build. The robber who had threatened him was impatient and aggressive.

Finally, the train moved forward, pulling just the two front coaches — the steam pipe and concertina covering connecting these to the rest of the train ripped apart. The rest of the train remained stationary on the track, its dozens of postal workers oblivious to the drama unfolding further down the line.

Mills was directed to stop at a white marker at Bridego Bridge, a few hundred yards down the line. The moment the train stopped Mills was taken back to Whitby and, handcuffed together, the two men were forced to lie face down on the embankment.

Two men stood guard over them. One repeated the offer of 'a few quid when this is all over', but warned them to keep quiet. 'There are some right bastards here,' he said.

The other told them they could smoke if they wanted. Whitby managed to get at his cigarettes one-handed and the second robber cadged one off him. Whitby said in evidence later that as he was lighting up he saw an army lorry and a Land Rover beside the bridge on the road below. He saw the robbers forming a human chain to lug the mailbags from the HVP carriage to the waiting flat-back wagon.

When the robbers had finished they hauled the driver and fireman into the HVP carriage and pushed them to the floor beside the sorters. After the robber's warning they remained on the floor, too frightened to move, until long after the gang of thieves had gone.

Frank Dewhurst, the postman in charge of the carriage, did stir after about 15 minutes, climbing carefully down onto the track. Seeing no robber left on guard he went back to the carriage and sent two of his men to use the phone at a nearby farm, not knowing that all the telephone lines in the area had been cut.

Meanwhile, back down the line the guard, Thomas Miller, age 61, had thought little of it when the train slowed then stopped. It had happened a number of times on the journey, as it did on every journey. But then he noticed from the gauge in his van that the vacuum had been released from the brake system. He climbed down and walked up to the engine to find out what was wrong. Except there was no engine: his train ended after 10 coaches.

There was a standard procedure to be followed when a train was stalled on a line. To prevent following trains crashing into it, detonators and red lamps needed to be set behind the train. Miller walked 1,000 yards back down the lines to lay them on the rails. Then he made his way forward to find the engine and the first two carriages.

At Bridego Bridge he found his colleagues and the postal workers in the HVP carriage. Several of them joined him to wave down a slow train travelling south on a different track. They took it to Cheddington Station, where they phoned Euston to tell of the theft. The duty officer there called Scotland Yard. The Metropolitan Police in turn contacted the Buckinghamshire Constabulary headquarters in Aylesbury.

It was 90 minutes since the robbery and the thieves had long since returned to their hide-out with their loot.

A QUESTION OF TIMING

The robbery was planned like a military operation, and indeed all of the robbers wore military uniforms of some kind or another. They had set out from their temporary base, 27 miles due west of Bridego Bridge, at 12.30 am in two Land Rovers and an ex-army lorry: if anyone had seen them, they would have assumed they were an army convoy. But they were keen to avoid attention. The farmhouse they had rented, Leatherslade Farm, was up an unpaved track off a B-road just outside the village of Oakley in Oxfordshire, and they had charted a route to the bridge that would avoid all major roads and large towns.

The robbers drove slowly so as not to be noticed, and it took them one hour to reach the bridge. Parking the vehicles near the bridge, they set a white marker on the track, then broke into a workman's hut and took pickaxes and a long crowbar, before cutting the telephone wires either side of the track and those in nearby fields that led to local farmhouses.

The success of the robbers' plan depended, of course, on their ability to stop the train. Three of them now took one of the Land Rovers along the road that ran parallel to the railway track to the warning signal, known as a dwarf signal, and the main signal. They carried with them batteries, leads, clips — and a pair of gloves.

The other robbers were spread out along the length of the track on either side of the rails. They had two walkie-talkies and torches in case the radios failed. By 2.50 am everyone was in position and all the preparations had been completed.

Just after 3 am the train came down the track. A member of the gang at the dwarf signal attached the amber light to batteries with clips and put one of the gloves over the green light. At the main signal, another robber did the same with the other glove and switched on the red light now attached to batteries (see plate 1).

Once the train had stopped and Mills and Whitby had been subdued, the robbers uncoupled the HVP carriage from the one behind it and detached the vacuum pipe between them.

They carried no guns. Several of them later claimed that what the postal workers heard as 'get the guns' was actually 'get the c*nts'.

They had their own driver, never identified but most likely to have been a retired railworker. However, when it came to it, he couldn't move the train forward, either out of nerves (he is said to have been distressed by the sight of Mills's bloodied face) or because he was unfamiliar with this particular English Electric locomotive. That was why Mills was called into service at the last moment.

The thieves were working to a strict timetable, so strict that they didn't take those last seven HVP bags and didn't stop to pick up an eighth that had been dropped on the embankment. They had 120 mailbags crammed into the flat-bottomed lorry.

The convoy set out again once the robbers had taken off their boiler suits and balaclavas. Their route took them through Wingrave, Aston Abbots, Cublington, Whitchurch, Oving Pitch-cott, Upper Winchendon and Chilton. They didn't see another vehicle until the small convoy was about to join the road from Long Crendon to Oakley when two cars went by.

Throughout their journey they had a VHF radio tuned into the frequency of the Buckinghamshire Constabulary, but no messages came over it about the robbery or, indeed, anything else. Bruce Reynolds later claimed that the men in the lorry sang along to Tony Bennett on the radio singing 'The Good Life', but that might be just colourful embellishment.

A few minutes after the two cars had passed, the convoy turned onto the track leading up to Leatherslade Farm, which was concealed from view from the road by the trees surrounding it. As the robbers pulled up in front of the ramshackle farmhouse, at 4.30 am, the VHF radio burst into life with a call to all cars, reporting that a train had been robbed near Linslade. Or, as the same fanciful robber had it: 'You won't believe this,' said one officer over the airwaves, 'but they've just stolen a train.'

Not quite a train: just two million, six hundred and thirty-one thousand, six hundred and eighty-four pounds.

CHAPTER TWO

A Motley Crew

The men who returned to Leatherslade Farm after this most audacious of robberies were in fact a motley crew of professional London criminals. Some were small-time crooks, brought in simply to help shift the mailbags from train to lorry. Ironically, Ronnie Biggs, now probably the best known of all the robbers, falls into this category.

They were led, as best we can tell, by Bruce Reynolds, working closely with his friends Gordon Goody and Charlie Wilson. These three were 'high-end' professional thieves who apparently made a good living out of stealing. (I say apparently because whilst Reynolds was known for driving flash sports cars and holidaying in the south of France, the other two lived quietly. Indeed, Goody lived with his mother in a cramped terraced house in Putney.)

Others, such as Buster Edwards, made a reasonable living from the proceeds of their mostly petty thievery. And yet others were muscle — 'the real bastards' Mills and Whitby were warned about.

The robbers who did the bulk of the planning were Bruce Reynolds, Charlie Wilson, Gordon Goody and Buster Edwards. Fordham called them 'the chiefs'. Almost 50 years and many testimonies after the Great Train Robbery, it's still not clear how many men they enlisted to rob the train.

According to the National Archives files, the police thought there were 15 men actually 'on the track' though 'many more' linked to the robbery (HO 287/1496). Others have suggested 17 on the track.

The mail workers in the carriage were only aware of the men who rushed the carriage. They did not know what was going on outside the carriage nor did they have any sense of the numbers involved. Driver Mills and fireman Whitby, lying on the embankment, were in a better position, but Mills was injured and Whitby had only a partial view.

The 11 robbers we know were on the track were (in alphabetical order, not order of importance) Ronnie Biggs, Roger Cordrey, Buster Edwards, Gordon Goody, Jim Hussey, Roy James, Bruce Reynolds, Bob Welch, Jimmy White, Charlie Wilson and Tommy Wisbey. John Daly, Reynolds's brother-in-law, was believed to be part of the conspiracy and on the track, but he was acquitted at the first trial of the robbers because the fingerprint evidence against him did not hold up.

THE FOUR MAIN PLAYERS

Bruce Reynolds was one of the most charismatic of the bunch. Often referred to as a natural leader, he was tall and good-looking. He had a raffish fondness for fast cars and stylish clothes, but this was offset by his spectacles, which gave him a scholarly appearance.

He was a Battersea boy, born in September 1931, son of an ardent trade unionist who worked at Ford's Dagenham car factory. A romantic and something of a fantasist, he saw himself at first as a Raffles-type thief then, for the Great Train Robbery, as the leader of a unit carrying out some heroic World War II military operation behind enemy lines.

He'd left school at 14 and by 1948 had not been able to hold down any job for longer than a few weeks. After his first stint in borstal in 1949 he never really had a job, petty theft alternating with frequent spells first in borstal then in prison.

As a joke someone once referred to him in a pub as 'the youngest major in the British army' and he played up to this. In fact, his army career lasted scarcely 48 hours before he went absent without leave. According to police files, he had joined the Royal Army Medical Corps as a private on 1 May 1952. On 4 May he decamped from his unit. He was arrested on 27 May and handed back. On 11 June he went over the wall again to resume his criminal life. Arrested in October and charged in November with shop breaking and car theft, he was immediately discharged from the army for misconduct.

Reynolds had a reputation for doing top-class crime, but the 11 previous convictions recorded by the police when he eventually came to trial for the train robbery were all for minor things, including stealing from a shop display and receiving a stolen heat lamp. (Most bizarrely, a couple of months before the Great Train Robbery, on 30 May 1963, he was fined in court in Ongar for poaching.)

But when he was out of prison he did somehow manage to live a lavish lifestyle. He avoided the regular criminal drinking clubs and pubs, preferring to be seen in the posh hotels and restaurants up town.

He had known Charlie Wilson since they were boys in Battersea and had done a couple of jobs with Buster Edwards, whom he had met — according to biographer Piers Paul Read — at the Shirley Ann, a club run by the Richardson 'firm'. In 1961, when he was 30, he married Frances, the 16-year-old sister of a former lover. He and Frances had a son, Nicholas.

Charlie Wilson, born on 30 June 1932, was a big, cheerful man with a quick sense of humour. He lived in Clapham with his wife and three daughters. Piers Paul Read stated that he was friends with 'certain violent and unscrupulous gangsters who ran the protection rackets in the West End' and, further, that he would 'blow off the legs or head of an adversary with a sawn-off shotgun without asking why'. However, the author offers no evidence for this and there is nothing in the court transcripts or police records to support the claims.

Wilson's criminal record is distinctly small time: stealing petrol, car theft, intent to steal from a car, receiving stolen goods and conspiracy to steal, for which he got his longest prison term of 30 months. However, as with Reynolds, it is perhaps the things for which he was never caught that most clearly mark the man.

He kept up a respectable working-man front. When he was released from that 30 months' prison sentence in 1961 he took a job as a window-cleaner, then became a driver at Spitalfields Market. In 1962 he opened a drinking club—The Charter-house—in nearby Smithfields, but soon after went into his father-in-law's greengrocery business in Penge.

There is a memo of instruction to counsel in the archive (ASSI 13/643) which either sheds a prosaic light on his friendship with another robber, Roy James, or was made up simply to demonstrate how lacking in criminal intent their friendship was. It states that the two men had known each other for 10 or 11 years before the robbery. Between 1955 and 1957 they used to go to Wimbledon Palais together twice a week, often accompanied by Wilson's future wife. Although they were in the same prison between 1957 and 1960, the note states that they only met again in 1960 in a cinema queue and started seeing each other once a month thereafter.

The third main player in the planning of the robbery was Douglas Gordon Goody, born in March 1930, who Peta Fordham places at the centre of her book about the robbers. Her portrayal of Goody is colourfully written. She describes him as 'a man of cold courage and sardonic humour, a more than life-size figure, with nerves of steel and the wolfish handsomeness of the pack leader that in fact he is.'

This man of cold courage, this pack leader, in his early thirties, lived with his mum in a small house in Putney in a tiny bedroom and had on one arm the tattoo 'Hello Ireland', on the other 'Dear Mother'.

Piers Paul Read described him as 'a huge man with a thin face and a crafty smile'. He also said that he was 'avaricious, lazy, frightening'.

Goody, as we shall see, was undoubtedly attractive to women, whom he liked to take to posh restaurants in the West End. Left to himself, his habits were different: he preferred to drink in the quiet pubs of Putney.

He had the typical teenage years of the professional criminal. Aged 15, he was poaching and stealing bikes. Aged 16, he was sent to borstal for receiving a stolen jersey. In 1948 he was back in borstal for chucking a stone through a plate glass window to steal cigarettes and clothes. He got his first proper gaol term almost as soon as he got out for robbing and beating up a gay man he said had made advances to him. He also got 12 strokes of the birch. And in 1956 he was back in gaol for a failed jewel robbery in Ireland. His next appearance in police records might indicate that he had upped his game: in 1961 he was fined for possession of a firearm and ammunition.

In that year, Read states, he teamed up with Buster Edwards for the first time to carry out several robberies. They started with bookies and the odd wages snatch, then attempted and failed to do a biggish job in Cork. Edwards temporarily joined another firm for a West End bank job that went wrong and a wages snatch that went better. Then he and Goody got back together for another wages snatch, and this time Goody invited Charlie Wilson to join them. Goody's given trade was that of a hairdresser.

Ronald Christopher 'Buster' Edwards is perhaps the most complex of the robbers. Portrayed in the eighties film *Buster* by rock star Phil Collins as a cockney cheeky chappie who meant no harm and enjoyed a laugh, Edwards was a former boxer whose favoured weapon was, apparently, an iron bar — he confessed to being the one who hit Mills the train driver (though other robbers denied this claim). Born on 27 January 1932 in London, from 1956 he is purported to have been part of a crime firm run by the Kray brothers' enforcer Freddie Foreman, alongside fellow Great Train Robber Tommy Wisbey.

THE REST OF THE GANG

Thomas William Wisbey, born April 1930, was a minor member of the robbery gang. He was a bookmaker who had nothing on his criminal record except a stint in borstal when he was 17 for shopbreaking and a four-month prison sentence. He had served his time in 1958 for receiving stolen wireless sets.

Wisbey, like many of the Great Train Robbers, had informal links to the two main criminal gangs that dominated London in the sixties: the Krays and the Richardsons. Freddie Foreman, a hard case who was an enforcer for the Krays — implicated in the notorious murders of Jack 'The Hat' McVitie and Ginger Marks — claimed that Edwards and Wisbey had invited him to take part in the Great Train Robbery, but he turned them down (Foreman, *Brown Bread Fred*).

Another notorious sixties villain, Mad Frankie Fraser, who worked with the Richardsons, claimed that Wisbey had invited him to join the Great Train Robbery team too. Fraser said he actually went down to their hide-out at Leatherslade Farm, but 'it was decided quite wisely that I shouldn't take part. I was on the run at the time and red hot. The police had put me on Police 5' (Fraser and Morton, *Mad Frank & Mad Frank and Friends Omnibus*). Many years later Fraser was to marry Wisbey's daughter, Marilyn.

Roy James, born in Fulham in August 1935, is perhaps the most tragic of the Great Train Robbers. He could have been an internationally famous racing driver, but instead chose crime and lost everything. Between 1948 and 1960 he served seven prison terms for shopbreaking, burglary, car theft and, on one occasion, even stealing three pairs of trousers from a shop's display stand (this, bizarrely, was a type of theft that a number of the robbers had in common).

He learned silversmithing in prison, but when he came out in 1960 he got a job as a milkman, then as a driver up in Soho. Two years later he rented a garage in Battersea to operate as a mechanic. By now he had discovered the new sport of go-karting. He thrived, switched to motor-racing, found he was a natural and won several international races. His photograph appeared in the newspapers, he was interviewed on television and he attracted a sponsor. However, he would not shake his criminal past.

According to Piers Paul Read, with his friend Mickey Ball, James had stolen Jaguars for smash-and-grab, then moved on to cat burglary. In 1962 the two men had spent an extravagant three months on the Côte d'Azur and stolen almost £150,000 worth of jewellery whilst they were there.

Brian Field was born in December 1934 and was immediately put up for adoption. He served two years in the Royal Army Service Corps, seeing service in Korea. When discharged from the military it was with 'a very good character'. He and his German wife enjoyed the good life. He had no qualms about cutting corners in his job as a solicitor's clerk in order to live it.

Jim Hussey was stealing pencils and sports equipment in 1946, aged 13. He had moved on to cars by the time he was 16, at 17 he was imprisoned for grievous bodily harm and assault, and he was always ready thereafter to use violence. In 1958, after a number of petty crimes, he was imprisoned for stealing cigarettes and tobacco worth almost £11,000 from a warehouse and for causing grievous bodily harm whilst resisting arrest. Oddly, his most recent crime had been as part of a gang of pick-pockets who had gone to Munich to try their luck. Soon caught, they had spent five months in a German gaol before being deported. His given occupation was painter and decorator.

Bob Welch, born in March 1929, ran the New Crown Club in the Elephant and Castle, London. His record was pretty clean, although in 1958 he had been imprisoned for receiving stolen custard powder. A lot of custard powder: it was valued, along-side stolen tea and coffee, at over £2,500.

Roger Cordrey was pretty clean, too. Born in May 1922, he was actually a florist in Brighton by trade. He had convictions for embezzlement and falsification of accounts back in 1941, but was essentially in the gang because of his knowledge of trains and the railway network.

Jimmy White, an ex-paratrooper, was an old thief who Reynolds worked with often and who may have been involved in the airport job mentioned below. According to Read, Reynolds used him as his 'quartermaster'. Ronnie Biggs was an after-thought. A petty thief who had spent far more time in prison than out of it, he started out in 1945 stealing pencils and by 1956 hadn't got much further than stealing paint and a pedal cycle. He was an opportunistic thief who made a reasonable living at his straight job as a handyman.

According to his friend Bruce Reynolds, Biggs was approached because he knew a retired train driver the gang thought they would need in the robbery. However, the petty thief then asked if he could come along as well.

Bill Boal was almost 50 at the time of the robbery. He seems to have been a man on the very fringes of crime through his friendship with Roger Cordrey. He had earned a police record in1947 and 1949 for minor things such as receiving stolen money and fiddling an electricity meter. (Although in April 1963 he had been convicted of assault on a policeman.) Reynolds is adamant in his autobiography that he had never met Boal, that indeed the first he heard of him was when Cordrey and Boal were arrested soon after the robbery. Boal was not involved in the planning nor the execution of the crime. The police and the court, unfortunately for Boal, were later to believe otherwise.

All accounts of the preparation for and execution of the robbery refer to other men involved in the robbery who were never identified. Piers Paul Read gives one of them the false name 'Bill Jennings' and both he Reynolds call another one 'Frank Munroe'. The retired train driver brought in to move the train along is referred to variously as 'Stan' or 'Peter'.

THE BEGINNINGS OF A PLAN

As we have seen, most of the robbers had form and most had worked with each other in some combination before. Piers Paul

Read contends that they were in fact two separate London gangs amalgamated for the purposes of the robbery and that there was rivalry between them, but Reynolds in his autobiography denies this rivalry. The police records in the Archives are frustratingly silent on most of the background links between the robbers.

Late in 1962, the real nucleus of the train robbery gang worked together on an ambitious heist from London airport's Comet House. Charlie Wilson, Gordon Goody, Buster Edwards and Bruce Reynolds put together a team that included future train robber Roy James to snatch a £62,000 payroll whilst dressed as city gents to allay suspicion.

The Flying Squad, the cross-boundary branch of London's Metropolitan Police Service, whose task was to detect and prevent such crimes, guessed who some of the robbers were and pulled in Charlie Wilson, Gordon Goody and Roy James —although only Wilson and Goody were formally charged. At the Old Bailey trial Wilson was acquitted after the prosecution had given its evidence and the jury could not agree on Goody's guilt (he later claimed to have bribed a juror). Goody's guilt or innocence hinged on whether or not a hat, submitted as evidence in court, belonged to him. At the retrial he was acquitted because when he tried the hat on it fell over his ears. According to some sources he had bribed a policeman to exchange the original hat for an identical one that was several sizes larger.

The robbers were now 'in the money'. Roy James is said to have used his share of the take to buy a Brabham racing car, but some of their ill-gotten gains were also used to fund preparations for the Great Train Robbery. Although there was probably no mastermind behind the robbery there was certainly somebody who had the inside information about the money on the night train. Indeed, it is assumed that such a person was on the railway station in Glasgow to let the robbers know by telephone when the train set out on its journey south. This person, who has never been identified, is usually described as the Ulsterman (in Piers Paul Read's *The Train Robbers* and Reynolds' autobiography). According to Read, it was after the London airport robbery that the Ulsterman approached solicitor's clerk Brian Field and offered the robbers the mail train hijack. Field in turn told Gordon Goody, whom he had represented in the past.

In Read's account, Goody and Edwards went to Field's office and were taken by a go-between called Mark to meet an 'ordinary, slightly balding, middle-aged man' in Finsbury Park. This man knew all about the HVP train. Goody and Edwards then told Reynolds and Wilson.

The four men began their research and brought in others, including Roy James as getaway driver, and a 'heavy' they had intended to use on the airport job, Jim Hussey.

Buster Edwards had been living under a false name in a Twickenham flat since 1962. Here the gang met to pull together a plan. Police discovered after the robbery that neighbours had been aware of about eight men visiting almost every day in the couple of weeks before the robbery. They came in groups of two or three.

The thing that kept coming up in the planning was how, exactly, they were going to stop the train at the right spot to be able to rob it and get away. After a number of journeys up and down the line within an hour or so of London, they identified the spot—Bridego Bridge. But the burning question remained. How were the gang to stop the train?

There were precedents of a sort. A criminal gang had been robbing trains on the London–Brighton line for a couple of years prior to the Great Train Robbery, although these were pretty much opportunistic thefts. On these occasions, a handful of men would hang around near the guard's van. After they had distracted the guard, the crooks would steal whatever registered mail was to hand, without having any guarantee of the value of the contents.

Roger Cordrey was the member of this gang who had figured out that the most effective way to distract the guard—and provide themselves with a getaway—was to stop a train in its tracks by changing the signal lights to red.

Edwards's old partner in crime Tommy Wisbey (if Freddie Foreman is to be believed) was also a member of this gang, as was a man called Bob Welch. Edwards proposed bringing this gang in on the night train robbery.

PREPARATIONS CONTINUE...

Jimmy White, calling himself Bentley, bought one of the Land Rovers and the lorry in early August. The other Land Rover was stolen from central London. Both were given identical number plates. (Edwards's neighbours in Twickenham actually saw one of these vehicles outside his flat on Wednesday 7 August.)

Reynolds decided they would cause less of a stir if they dressed as military men in an area where there were a number of military encampments. Fatigues, balaclavas, sleeping bags, torches and other kit—including walkie-talkies for when they were strung out along the track and a VHF receiver to monitor police transmissions—were purchased. For himself Reynolds bought a major's crowns to go on an Airborne Forces smock and the SAS winged dagger to go on his beret.

According to Reynolds, the robbers carried out 'a low-key rehearsal' at Stewarts Lane depot near Nine Elms in Battersea. The decision was made to hide out relatively near the scene of the crime to avoid the risk of running police roadblocks. Leatherslade Farm was selected (see plate 4). It was in the next county, around 30 minutes' drive away by back roads and country lanes. The nearest reasonable sized town to the farm was Thame.

Brian Field brought in Leonard Field (no relation), a merchant seaman, to act as front-person in the purchase of the farm. He also had to involve his boss, a straight-down-the-line solicitor, John Wheater, in the purchase. Whilst Leonard Field, whose brother had been inside, knew something crooked was going down, Wheater appears to have been duped.

Two of the robbers—Gordon Goody and Ronnie Biggs—went out of their way to get alibis that proved to be more trouble than they were worth. Goody had gone to Ireland with his mother and a friend on 2 August and intended his alibi to be that he was still there at the time of the robbery. Unfortunately for Goody, however, there was solid evidence that he had returned to England on 6 August.

Biggs told his wife, Charmian, he was going off on a wood-cutting job for a few days in Wiltshire. His misfortune was that his brother died on the first night he left home. His wife asked the police to find him in Wiltshire to give him the sad news. The police went to where Biggs said he would be. When he wasn't there they checked every other wood-cutting site in the county, destroying his alibi in the process.

According to Reynolds, the robbers arrived at the farm in small groups on 6 August ready to do the job in the early morning hours of 7 August. First to arrive was Reynolds with Edwards, Jimmy White, Biggs and 'Stan/Peter', the train driver. Last to arrive was Gordon Goody, at 11 pm, a bottle of whiskey in his hand, to say the Ulsterman had phoned to postpone the job by 24 hours. Fordham also states that the job was delayed by 24 hours. Finally, at 11 pm on the evening of 7 August, the robbers got into their uniforms and set off for Sears Crossing.

It had been a poor summer, but the evening was mild when they set out, equally mild when they returned. The Land Rovers and the lorry would have made a racket on the quiet roads the robbers chose as their route, but there was — apparently — no one to hear them. This motley crew did not know it yet, but they were about to pull off the crime of the century. They would do it almost flawlessly. And then they would go on to blow it.

CHAPTER THREE

Farm Hideaway

When the robbers arrived back at Leatherslade Farm they were euphoric and exhausted. They immediately off-loaded the bags and stacked them along the living room wall and along the hallway. The lorry was backed into a shed and the Land Rovers parked in a lock-up garage.

Reynolds said that everyone immediately started ripping open the bags and stacking the packages inside, with Goody checking the bags for homing devices.

In Read's account one of the unidentified robbers went upstairs and fell straight asleep on his air bed. Gordon Goody positioned himself by the window with a pair of binoculars, a radio and a bottle of whiskey. Tommy Wisbey set to, opening all the mail sacks in the kitchen and tossing the packages into the living room where Charlie Wilson and Buster Edwards opened them. Roger Cordrey then stacked the money in piles of five pound, one pound and 10-shilling notes. There was a separate pile for Irish and Scottish money.

The fivers were in £2,500 bundles, the one pounds in £500

bundles and the 10-shilling notes in £250 bundles. Since the packets weighed around two tons in total, that was a lot of work for just four men.

Ronnie Biggs, in his *Sun* newspaper account (DPP 2/4849) said that he and Charlie Wilson counted and stacked the money, with Wilson doing the twist, singing 'I like it, I like it', the recent chart-topper by Gerry and the Pacemakers. He reckoned the work was done by lunchtime. They counted roughly £1,200,000 in five pound notes and £1,300,000 in one pound and 10-shilling notes. Total around £2,500,000.

The exact total is said to have been £2,631,684. However, the 1965 official police report about the crime by E.J. Dodds stated that £2,595,997-10s-0d had been stolen. Either way, all but 1,579 of the notes were untraceable. The Midland Bank had even worse news: it hadn't insured the banknote shipment so had to carry its half a million pound loss itself.

The robbers were elated. Rather than doing the twist, Read has Charlie Wilson jumping up and down, pointing at a pile of money and saying: 'Look at that Bobbikins. There's eighty grand in that pile.' Old pound notes and 10-shilling notes were used to light cigarettes and cigars and there's an enduring story that some of the robbers played the board game Monopoly with real money. It was Ronnie Biggs's birthday so they each solemnly gave him a fiver.

Seeing the money piled up in their hideaway was the high-point for the thieves, although they didn't know it yet. For

Leatherslade Farm is where a perfectly planned, almost perfectly executed crime fell apart. This motley crew of small-timers had committed a robbery that there was every chance they could get clear away with. (As several of them probably did.) But they blew it in their farm hideaway.

THE SPLIT

Reynolds in his autobiography passes over the division of the spoils. Read's breakdown of the split—who got 'whacks' and who merely got 'drinks'—has its own Appendix. He suggests 17 robbers got £150,000 each.

This seems more accurate than his fanciful account in the body of the book of Otto Skorzeny creaming off £1,000,000, leaving £90,000 per robber. However, it doesn't take into account what the person who came up with the scheme would have got. It also assumes everyone got an equal share.

Biggs said there were 17 equal 'whacks' plus £20,000 to the train driver—Peter/Stan—they took along but didn't use (he calls him Fred, just to complicate things further). Biggs said he got £115,000 in one pound notes and £43,000 in fivers, totalling £158,000. Later, in one of her newspaper articles, his wife Charmian said he only got £120,000. Biggs also suggested that nobody could be bothered with the 10-shilling notes so Reynolds took most of those.

Fordham reckoned that 'the main four'—presumably Goody,

Wilson, Reynolds and Edwards — got £250,000 each; the main 'labourers' £100,000; lesser helpers smaller amounts. Later, at the trial of Roy James, a piece of paper, not in his handwriting, was produced. It had been found in his holdall when he had been arrested. On it were the following notations:

1st, 22,500 = 5.
2nd, 15,000 = 1.
3rd, 18,200 = 1.
4th, 6,800 = 1.
5th. 14,000 = 5.

The total is £225,900. The prosecution assumed this was a partial record of the split.

In his memoirs the then head of the Flying Squad, George Hatherill, has 18 not 17 shares. He says that the division began when the gang reached the farm. This was easy because the cash was in packets, with the amount stated on the wrapper. There were 18 shares of around £140,000. At noon, the share-out was done.

He further stated:

Only 14 men had been concerned in the actual hold-up; the remaining four shares were for others who had been concerned in preparations for the robbery or had been bribed to give vital information.

1 *Left:* The signal at Sears Crossing that stopped the mail train. Note the glove that was used to mask the green light and the battery used to turn on the red. (HO 242/2)

2 *Below:* Interior of the High Value Package carriage, stripped bare by the robbers. (HO 242/2)

MESSAGE			Time	TEXT OF MESSAGE	
om	To	File No.			
	5&3		0426	Go to Cheddington Rail. Stat. emergency, ambulance on way	
		✓		perhaps break.	
	4	✓	0428	Go to Bletchley Rail. Stat. re above – no details yet	
	4, 5, 3	VA	0436	A short while ago whilst train was stationary at Cheddington	
				Rail. Stat. fireman stoker and G.P.O. employees attacked and	
		✓		property stolen – no other details known	
5	3		0441	At Rail Stat. 30 men involved in cars and lorries employees	
		✓		handcuffed all Royal Mail gone – no desc of veh. or men.	
	15	✓	0447	Road at High Wycombe junction A40 and A4010	
			0448	Occurred at 0315 hrs number of men 30-50 some armed, in lorry and cars	
		✓		no desc.	
			0448	Hacksaw required at Royal Bucks Hospital, for injured who are	
		✓		handcuffed – American Type cuffs	
			0450	Train going South stopped 4 miles north of Cheddington location	
		✓	–	at Seer Crossing	
	44	✓	0452	Go to Cheddington Area	
8	VA (Bedfordshire)	✓	0453	All details as above	
	8	✓	0455	Patrol A5 toward Lt. Buzzard Area	
	45	✓	0455	Patrol your area Stewkley	
	56 (Dog Van)	✓	0456	Directions to scene	
	32	✓	0456	General Patrol – cover roads from area	
	11	✓	0456	Patrol Roads M1 leading from area	
		✓	0500	Pos. Men may be dressed in Railway Employees uniform	
8	VA	✓	0501	Re above	
1		✓	0502	Seer Crossing B.488 Linslade.	

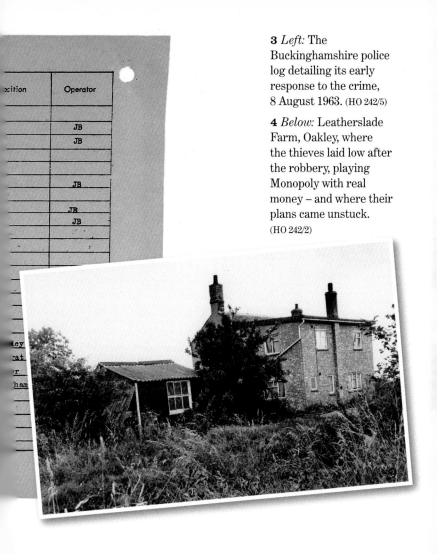

xition	Operator
	JB
	JB
	JB
	JB
	JB

3 *Left:* The Buckinghamshire police log detailing its early response to the crime, 8 August 1963. (HO 242/5)

4 *Below:* Leatherslade Farm, Oakley, where the thieves laid low after the robbery, playing Monopoly with real money – and where their plans came unstuck. (HO 242/2)

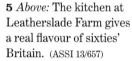

5 *Above:* The kitchen at Leatherslade Farm gives a real flavour of sixties' Britain. (ASSI 13/657)

6 *Left:* The farmhouse's larder, open to show the thorough, if basic, food provisioning by the robbers. (ASSI 13/657)

7 *Right:* Buckinghamshire police 'wanted' telegram for Bruce Reynolds, Charlie Wilson and Jimmy White. (HO 242/5)

DIVS — 1335
On.Co — 1343

Copies (2) t Op. Room

INDEX.   Indexed Cleared
Persons Wanted   24 (?)
            Suspected
            Missing
M. Value Stolen
            Suspected
Goods Stolen
            Found
M. Value Stock   pd   Q P 241

POLICE BUCKS
METPOL LDN
        EXPRESS MESSAGE NO.66/63 AND ALL PORT WARNING
TO ALL DISTRICTS AND ALL PORTS   FROM COMMISSIONER METPOL(C01)

    ON THE 8TH AUGUST 1963 AT SEARS CROSSING,CHEDDINGTON,BUCKS,
A NUMBER OF MEN STOPPED AN EXPRESS TRAVELLING POST OFFICE AND STOLE
APPROXIMATELY 2.1/4 MILLION POUNDS STERLING.

    THE FOLLOWING THREE MEN ARE WANTED FOR PARTICIPATION IN THIS
OFFENCE:-

1. BRUCE RICHARD REYNOLDS. CRO 41212/48 AGED 31 YEARS A MOTOR
DEALER OR ANTIQUE DEALER.6'1'' PROP. BUILD. FRESH SLIGHTLY
SUN-TANNED COMP. LIGHT BROWN HAIR, GREY EYES. SPEAKS WITH A
QUIET COCKNEY ACCENT. HE HAS A SLIGHT CLEFT IN HIS CHIN AND
WEARS EITHER HORN-RIMMED OR RIMLESS SPECTACLES.

2. CHARLES FREDERICK WILSON CRO 5010/54 AGED 31 YEARS A TURF
ACCOUNTANT, 6' TALL, SLIM BUILD, FRESH COMP. DARK BROWN HAIR,
BLUE EYES, SCAR ON KNUCKLE OF THE FIRST FINGER OF HIS LEFT HAND.
HAS A COCKNEY ACCENT.

3. JAMES E. WHITE. CRO 26113/55 AGED 43 YEARS, A CAFE PROPRIETOR

5'10'' SLIM BUILD, SALLOW COMP. BROWN STARING EYES, BROWN HAIR,
RECEDING AT THE TEMPLES, WITH SLIGHT QUIFF IN THE CENTRE.
REASONABLY WELL SPOKEN. HAS RECENTLY REMOVED A SMALL MOUSTACHE
HE HAS HAD FOR SOME TIME. MAY BE ACCOMPANIED BY A WOMAN, WHOSE
NAME IS THOUGHT TO BE '' SHERREE'' A BABY APPROXIMATELY SIX
MONTHS OLD, AND A WHITE MINIATURE POODLE CALLED ' GIGI'

ANY INFORMATION CONCERNING ANY OF THESE PERSONS PLEASE
COMMUNICATE WITH OPERATIONS ROOM, AYLESBURY POLICE HEADQUARTERS
TELEPHONE AYLESBURY 5010.

T OF O 12-20PM ++   =
POLICE BUCKS   1-36PM +++ FIN +?
R   1336 22 AUG 63 PC.241

WANTED—*continued.*

dealer trading as Max Antiques.—**JAMES EDWARD WHITE**, alias **JAMES BRYAN** and **JAMES EDWARD WHITEFOOT** (uses many aliases), C.R.O. No. 26113-55, Case 9,

James Edward White (photograph taken 19-5-59)

16-5-60, b. Paddington (L.) 21-2-20, cafe proprietor, 5ft. 10in., slim build, c. sallow, h. brown (receding at temples, slight quiff in centre), e. brown (staring), thin nose (slightly hooked), reasonably well spoken, has recently removed moustache which he has had for some time, Royal Artillery crest rt. forearm.   Cons. for larceny, receiving, shopbreaking, at Bedford and M.P. (S and T).

May be accompanied by woman, believed named Sherree, a baby about 6 mos. old and a white miniature poodle called Gigi.—**ROY JOHN JAMES**, nickname "**THE**

Roy John James (photograph taken 20-5-60)

WEASEL", C.R.O. No. 17638-56, b. (L.) 30-8-35, silversmith, 5ft. 4in., medium to slim build, c. fresh, h. lt. brown, e. hazel, long nose (thin).   Cons. for larceny, receiving, taking motor vehicle without consent, shopbreaking, dangerous driving, etc., at Jersey and M.P. (B, L, W and X).   Last, 13-6-63—fined.   Det. Chief Supt. Butler in case   Telephone : (Aylesbury 5010).

2

---

8 *Right:* Wanted notice for Jimmy White and Roy James, from the *Police Gazette*, 23 August 1963. Bruce Reynolds was shown on the previous page. (HO 287/1496)

9 *Facing:* Wanted notice for Buster Edwards and his wife June, from the *Police Gazette*, 12 September 1963. (HO 287/1496)

THE

POLICE  GAZETTE

PUBLISHED BY AUTHORITY.

NEW SERIES   THURSDAY, SEPTEMBER 12, 1963   No. 215, VOL. L

Matter for circulation under the headings "Commonwealth Citizens" or "Aliens" should be addressed "THE ALIENS REGISTRATION OFFICE, 10, PICCADILLY PLACE, W.1".

With all other manuscript for publication the envelope should be addressed "THE COMMISSIONER OF POLICE, NEW SCOTLAND YARD, S.W.1" with "C.R.O.(P.G.)" in top left corner.

JOSEPH SIMPSON,
The Commissioner of Police of the Metropolis.

Wanted

1.—Bucks., Aylesbury Co.—Robbery (mail train) vide Cases 1, 23-8-63 and 1, 30-8-63, etc.—RONALD EDWARDS, alias RONALD CHRISTOPHER EDWARDS and "BUSTER", C.R.O. No. 33535-61, D.C.R. No. 92069, b. London 27-1-31, florist/

club owner, 5ft. 6in., stocky build, c. fresh, h. dk. brown, e. brown, London accent, scar l. of nose, rt. forearm and below l. kneecap. Cons. for attempted larceny, assault on police, driving while disqualified, etc., at M.P. (B and M). Last, 21-11-61—14 days impt., etc. Passport No. 800944 issued 3-8-63.

May be accompanied by wife JUNE ROSE EDWARDS nee ROTHERY (passport No. 800945 issued 3-8-63), b. 31-8-32, 5ft. 3in., h. black, and daughter Nicolette, age 2yrs. 9 mos.

Believed to be travelling on Continent.

10 *Left:* The banknotes to a value of £30,440 concealed within the wall of Jimmy White's caravan in Reigate. (HO 242/2)

11 *Below:* One of the recovered bags of money photographed by the Buckinghamshire Police. (ASSI 13/657)

Quite how he reached these numbers is not clear. There is nothing in the official police files about this share-out of the loot. Since Hatherill also felt that a woman must have been part of the gang as only a woman would have been able to provision the kitchen of Leatherslade Farm so well (see p. 59), it's hard to decide what weight to give to his judgements.

SAFE HAVEN OR TRAP?

It is unclear how long the robbers had originally intended to hole up at Leatherslade Farm, but the consensus in the various accounts is that they were going to stay until the weekend. Certainly they had more than enough provisions for that. Indeed, the gang could comfortably have stayed for a couple of weeks or so, if necessary.

The food inventory the police later made is a snapshot of working-class eating habits of the time. It included 18 tins of luncheon meat, 9 tins of corned beef, 40 tins of baked beans, 18 pounds of butter, 20 tins of peas, 38 tins of soup, 15 tins of condensed milk, 34 tins of fruit salad, 32 pounds of sugar, 7 loaves and 19 cans of beer. Then there was cheese, Oxo, Bovril, biscuits, cakes, jam, coffee and a seductive bottle of ketchup — the use of which snared at least two of the robbers (see plates 5 and 6).

There was also a half a sack of potatoes, a barrel of apples and a case of oranges. Other gear later left behind included candles, gas stoves, 17 rolls of toilet paper, 11 inflatable rubber mattresses, blankets, pillows, 6 sleeping bags, 20 jackets, 9 pull-overs, some denim trousers and 20 towels.

Two things determined the robbers to leave earlier. Reynolds and Biggs both wrote that they passed nobody on their return to the farm after the robbery, but Reynolds said that en route to Sears Crossing the convoy had passed a solitary hitchhiker, an airman. Read had them passing this airman on the way back from the robbery.

According to Reynolds, the day after the robbery the news was broadcast on the radio that an airman hitching in the early hours of the morning had been passed by an army convoy. The police were very interested in this convoy.

On the day before the robbery, a local farmer, Mr Wyatt, had visited the farm to ask the new owners about continuing to rent fields belonging to Leatherslade. Reynolds pretended to be a works supervisor and said he would put in a word with the owners. That evening, Wyatt's son had come back and seen the gang's army lorry. Now Reynolds worried that the Wyatts would connect the lorry to the radio broadcast. The gang agreed that the lorry and Land Rovers could not be used again.

The robbers decided to split up with their shares of the loot, but there was the logistical problem of shifting all the money. What then followed was a farce, given the gang were hoping to slip away unnoticed, as cars came and went with increasing frequency.

Roger Cordrey left by bicycle on Thursday. He had made advance arrangements to rent a room in Oxford for that evening, but decided to stay in a hotel for a night. Cordrey made calls to Brian Field on behalf of Goody and Edwards. He also called a friend of Reynolds — Mary Manson — who had agreed to help him after the robbery, to let her know everyone would be leaving on Friday.

The rest of the robbers spent Thursday evening cleaning up the farm. Reynolds had insisted they wore gloves throughout their stay, but that hadn't always been feasible so now they wiped down all surfaces. They lit a bonfire in the garden and burned clothes and shoes, either there or in the kitchen stove. Attempts to burn the mailbags were less successful, so they dug a hole in the garden in which to bury them. The hole was big enough for only some bags and the balaclavas, so the rest of the mailbags were dumped in the cellar.

Although the robbers were cleaning up the consensus of opinion is that they had made arrangements to have the farm forensically cleaned — possibly even burned to the ground — at the weekend after they had gone. Biggs says Buster Edwards was supposed to contact a fellow London crook and offer him £40,000 to clean up, but there are, naturally, several variations on that story.

Roy James left next. According to Read, Brian Field and his German wife, Karin, arrived at Leatherslade Farm at dusk on Thursday evening and were asked to take James back to

London to buy two vans. Goody and Edwards intended to use these to transport the bulk of the money to Field's house near Pangbourne in Berkshire.

Reynolds says in his autobiography that he was first to leave on the sunny Friday morning. He walked down the lane to the bus stop dressed in sports jacket, cavalry twill trousers and chukka boots. Two 'colonel types' stopped to offer him a lift. In the car, conversation turned to the robbery. The driver suggested the robbers should be horse-whipped and Reynolds responded: 'That's right, sir — teach those blighters a lesson.'

This sounds like another of Reynolds's fanciful stories and what follows doesn't square with what the police discovered about his movements. He says he had a rendezvous with his friend Mary Manson in Thame. By this account she had a van for him that he drove back to the farm. He loaded 'two whacks' (his own and one for a robber he calls Paddy), returned to Thame to leave the van and the loot with Manson and caught the Greenline bus with Paddy to London. The two robbers took a cab from Victoria coach station to Manson's house in Mitcham and transferred the money to a lock up Reynolds had rented nearby. They hid the loot behind a stack of furniture.

There is a note in the police files that on this day Reynolds bought an Austin Healey sports car in the company of Mary Manson in Tring. Read has him buying two, then returning to the farmhouse in the evening with Mary Manson in her Ford Cortina. Just to complicate his movements further, there is a record of Reynolds ordering some shirts in Knightsbridge, too.

Gordon Goody was seen in Putney on Friday morning. Cordrey, meanwhile, had bought a second-hand Wolsey in Oxford. He returned to the farm for his money and to give Jimmy White a lift back into Oxford. After Cordrey dropped his money off in the room he'd rented, the two men went to Black Bourton to buy a Rover they'd seen advertised for sale in the morning paper. Cordrey took the Rover back to his new digs whilst White drove to Leatherslade Farm in the Wolsey. He passed it on to one of the unidentified robbers who went off to London in it.

By Friday evening the radio was reporting that the police believed the robbers were holed up somewhere within a 30-mile radius of Sears Crossing/Bridego Bridge and were searching all isolated properties.

According to Reynolds's own account, he was in London by now. According to Read, Reynolds, still at the farm, assigned one Austin Healey to Jimmy White, and Reynolds and Biggs used the second Healey. All drove to Biggs's flat in Redhill, where he discovered his wife had inadvertently blown his alibi. Biggs's account tells the same story about his wife and the alibi, except in his version there is no mention of other robbers and accomplices crowding into the flat.

At the trials later a neighbour, Mr Lawley, gave evidence that he had seen a black saloon head for the farm whilst a Mr Cunnington saw a small Riley van also head for the farm.

In Read's version, Field returned with two vans and the remaining robbers piled into those with their money and were taken to his house around 11.30 pm on the Friday evening. Brian Field's wife, Karin, later wrote an article for the German magazine *Stern*, saying that the gang did indeed come to her house on the Friday evening. She had to drive back to Leatherslade to take Roy James to Thame station so that he could get a train to London. She then led a convoy of the two vans back to her house. In Karin Field's version the gang stayed at her home for much of the weekend; girlfriends and wives arrived; there was a non stop party whilst sacks of money lay in piles all over the house. (This account of the article's contents appears in Peta Fordham's book.)

By midnight on Friday, whichever account or combination of accounts you choose to believe, all the robbers had vacated their hideaway. They left a farmhouse that was deserted but not empty. For in it was enough evidence to bring almost all the robbers down. The hideaway at Leatherslade Farm proved to be the robbers' undoing.

THE POLICE INVESTIGATION BEGINS

According to the Buckinghamshire Constabulary's control room log (see plate 3), the local police had arrived at the scene of the crime by around 4.30 am. A fireman on the slow line had driven the diesel with its two coaches to Cheddington Station.

Local police and an ambulance were waiting and driver Mills, still handcuffed to Whitby, had been taken to Aylesbury, where 17 stitches were put in his head.

Mills remained in hospital for two-and-a-half days. He had lacerated injuries to the back of his skull, which tends to support the contention that he was attacked from behind as he was struggling with someone in front. One of the cuts was 2 ½ inches long and ½ inch deep; there was another serious cut in front of his right ear plus smaller wounds.

The police had nothing to go on. The British Rail and GPO workers had no clue to the identity of the thieves. Whitby was the only witness to see a robber without a balaclava on — the man who had hailed him on the track — but could offer no description. Nor had the police any idea how much money had been stolen. In his memoirs George Hatherill, head of the Flying Squad, says that about an hour after he got to his office on the morning of the robbery he got an early edition of the evening paper in which the amount stolen was put at nearly £1,000,000.

Later that morning, the Chief Constable of Buckingham-shire, Brigadier John Cheney, circulated early details of the robbery to all police forces. His head of CID, DS Malcolm Fewtrell, was in nominal charge, but it was customary in those days to call in Scotland Yard for expert help. In London, Hath-erill, anticipating the call, sent for senior officers of the Flying Squad, the London and Provincial Crime Squad and the Intelligence Squad. Whilst they were meeting the formal request from Cheney came through.

That afternoon there was a top-level conference at the GPO in London. Fewtrell came down from Buckinghamshire to brief members of the GPO's Investigation Branch, the British Transport Police, Scotland Yard officers and Hatherill's élite team.

After that, Detective Chief Superintendent McArthur from Scotland Yard was put in effective charge, though in theory he was just an adviser to Brigadier Cheney. He liaised with Fewtrell and officers of the Railway Police CID and the GPO Investigation Branch.

The only leads came from Whitby, the fireman, and they were slight. He had told the police about the lorry and the Land Rover he had seen. He also thought one of the robbers had a cockney accent.

According to his memoir, Hatherill had already guessed these were London criminals. He also wondered whether they would have made a clean getaway or, knowing the police would set up roadblocks, have holed up somewhere nearby until the fuss died down. Hatherill claimed that, in light of the warning one of the robbers gave to the victims not to move for half an hour, he suggested to the conference at the GPO that there should be a systematic search of empty houses, farms, abandoned military camps etc within a 30mile radius of Sears Crossing. In a later internal police report reference was made to Hatherill's claim that he had made the suggestion at this meeting, but nobody could recollect him doing so.

> Commander Hatherill claims that at the meeting at the GPO
> Headquarters in London on the afternoon of the crime he
> mentioned this point but so far as can be ascertained no one
> else present at the meeting can remember his doing so.
>
> (HO 242/3)

Hatherill sent Chief Superintendent McArthur down to Buckinghamshire with a detective sergeant. Later there was criticism that it took 19 hours from the time of the crime to get just two Scotland Yard detectives down to the scene.

LEATHERSLADE FARM DISCOVERED

There was huge public interest in the case, and within days information was pouring into the incident room at the Buckinghamshire police headquarters in Aylesbury (see plate 14). Although the police had found no fingerprints when they dusted down every bit of the English Electric engine and the HVP coach, by Monday 12 August Macolm Fewtrell of Buckinghamshire CID had announced that the police believed the robbers were somewhere within a 30-mile radius of the robbery.

That day a farm labourer, John Maris, was working in a field by Leatherslade Farm when he took a peek through the hedge to see what the new owners were up to. According to Hatherill, he noted the windows were heavily curtained, but that a corner of each curtain was turned up so that anyone inside the house could peep out. His curiosity aroused, he went into the yard and saw a lorry in the shed and noted that the garage was locked. Back at his employer's house in nearby Oakley, John Maris called the police.

However, his was one of 400 calls logged in Aylesbury that day. Maris hung around, but no one came to see him. He phoned again on Tuesday 13 August. This time two policemen—Sergeant Blackman and Constable Wooley—were sent out from nearby Waddesdon police station. At the farm they clocked the lorry, broke into the garage and found the two Land Rovers. They noticed a half-dug hole and the remains of a bonfire round the front of the house.

The policemen forced a window and climbed into the farmhouse. First they saw the food stacked in the kitchen. There were potatoes and fruit piled under the stairs. Upstairs they found sleeping bags, air beds and blankets. Back downstairs they found the trap door to the cellar under the fruit and vegetables. Wooley went down and found mailbags and paper wrappers. His sergeant went to find a phone to alert his superiors in Aylesbury. Hatherill happened to be there that day. He, Fewtrell and Scotland Yard's McArthur drove out to the farm.

On arriving Fewtrell said: 'the whole place is one big clue'.

Back in Aylesbury, Hatherill held an impromptu press conference and journalists were allowed a quick look at Leatherslade before the police cordoned it off. On Wednesday 14 August, DS Maurice Ray and Scotland Yard's fingerprint department started work on the house.

Hatherill wrote that when the convoy of police arrived at the farmhouse he was surprised to discover a larder stacked like a supermarket. He commented, 'I felt pretty certain that a woman must have given advice about how the place should be equipped and stocked. Nothing, as far as I could see, had been forgotten...' At that stage Hatherill deduced that between 10 and 18 men had been holed up at the farm.

Neighbours in a nearby cottage had been aware of activity at the farm for some days. John Maris said he had been seeing vehicles and people coming and going since 29 July. A Mrs Nappin had heard vehicles on the night of the robbery. And the Wyatts, father and son, testified to what they had seen when they visited the farmhouse on the day before the robbery.

Hatherill decided to form special squads to deal with the various types of inquiry that would be needed, redeploying officers from various branches of the Yard. They included Chief Superintendent Tommy Butler from the CID (see plate 12). Butler was born in Shepherd's Bush and joined the Metropolitan Police, age 22, as PC965K, pounding a beat in Canning Town. After 15 years in the CID he was promoted to the Flying Squad. A workaholic who lived with his mother and never married, in the course of his career he was commended 32 times for 'brilliant work in detection'.

There are (of course) various versions of the way the robbers were identified. Fordham said McArthur at Scotland Yard had a call the day after the discovery of the farm in which all the main conspirators were named. Read believed Hatherill got the tip from a villain he visited in gaol. In his memoir, however, Hatherill is vague, but says it was almost three weeks before he began to receive a variety of information he could combine to form a comprehensive picture of the robbery and who had committed it.

Certainly it took 10 days to complete the task of dusting the farmhouse for prints — of which there were many. Then the Forensic Science Laboratory moved in. Whilst the fingerprint experts were meeting the pre-computer challenge of matching the photographs of the finger- and palm-prints they'd found with the hundreds of thousands of prints on file, the FSC experts were examining the farm buildings and absolutely everything in them.

By the time both teams had finished their work, the police were in a position to start naming names.

THE ROBBERS IN LIMBO

The robbers had been in something of a limbo. If you believe some of Read's account, the gang at the Fields' house had set out on their separate ways on the morning of Saturday 10 August. Tommy Wisbey, Bob Welch, Jim Hussey and an unidentified robber went to Reading where they paid cash for a second-hand car, a van and some suitcases, then, having loaded their money, set off for the south coast.

Racing driver Roy James came to get Charlie Wilson and another unidentified robber. They drove to Wilson's lock-up garage in the East End where Wilson and James left their loot. The unidentified robber drove off with his entire whack — and is never heard of in the public record again.

Read says that Goody stayed with the Fields until Sunday afternoon when the Ulsterman arrived and took his whack. Then Goody, too, went on his way.

There was some nervousness about the farmhouse being properly cleaned. Read's version is that Brian Field was supposed to take care of it, but on the Monday morning Charlie Wilson wasn't convinced that he had. Reynolds, Buster Edwards, Charlie Wilson and an unidentified robber met at teatime on Monday at Clapham North.

By this time, John Maris had made his telephone call to Buckinghamshire police headquarters.

The robbers decided they needed to get back to the farm and clean it themselves. According to Read, Edwards had left a pair of trousers, a pair of shoes and blankets from his flat in Twickenham at the house. This does not, however, square with an earlier part of Read's account in which he stated all old clothes were burned.

Read's account tells of these men meeting with Brian Field at Holland Park underground station on Tuesday morning. Field admits that the farm might not have been cleaned and the robbers make arrangements to go back later that day. En route, they hear on the radio that their hideaway has been discovered.

Then again … Reynolds says in his memoir that a day later, on Wednesday 13 August, he was worried the farm had not been cleaned up properly, so called a meeting outside a transport café on the North Circular. Edwards, Wilson and James attended and they decided to go back that night. Then Edwards bought a paper with the headline: 'Hide-out Discovered.' Actually, it doesn't matter which version is true. The essential fact is that once the farm was discovered everything changed. It was the beginning of the end.

CHAPTER FOUR

Game Over

When the farm was discovered, the robbers scattered. Bruce Reynolds, Jimmy White and Buster Edwards went into hiding. Gordon Goody tried to, though he knew that, like Charlie Wilson, the police would want to question him just on principle. If we accept there were two or three others on the track who were never caught, they successfully disappeared from the police radar forever.

The police struck lucky with the first robber to be arrested. Roger Cordrey had teamed up with his friend Bill Boal and together they'd gone down to Bristol. They came unstuck when, on the day the farm was discovered, Cordrey answered an advertisement for a garage to rent that had been placed by a policeman's widow. When he insisted on paying three months in advance in cash from a thick wad of notes she grew suspicious. She called the police, who arrived just as Cordrey and Boal were taking possession of the garage.

The police invited them to empty their pockets. They had about £270 between them and Boal had a receipt for the purchase of the Austin A35 that was in the garage. The car contained two bags stuffed with money and a pillowcase full of bank note wrappers. There was more money in a rented flat and in another car in another garage. The police found £850 in Cordrey's sister's house in London. Boal had £350 stashed away in his London home.

Altogether, the police recovered £141,000. Cordrey, his sister and brother-in-law, Bill Boal and his wife were all charged.

Charlie Wilson's fingerprints were the first to be identified by the police. He had left partial prints on the cellophane wrapping of a travel kit and on a drum of salt. His palm-print was on a window sill. At 1.36 pm on 22 August the Buckinghamshire police sent out a 'wanted' telegram for Bruce Reynolds, Charlie Wilson and Jimmy White (see plate 7). Charlie was arrested at home that day. According to arresting officer Tommy Butler's evidence in court, Wilson said: 'I do not see how you can make it stick without the poppy and you won't find that'. (In cockney rhyming slang 'poppy' is short for 'poppy red', rhymes with bread; 'bread and honey' rhymes with money.) Wilson denied forever after that he had made the remark.

Ronnie Biggs's fingerprints were the next to be identified. Hatherill says that his name had been passed to the police and his fingerprints on file checked against some of those found in the farmhouse. His prints were on Monopoly cards, a ketchup bottle and a Pyrex plate. He was arrested on 24 August, his situation made worse by the way in which his wife had managed innocently but irrevocably to wreck his alibi.

Hatherill had been given the names of Jim Hussey, Bob Welch and Tommy Wisbey. Hussey's prints were found on the tailboard of the lorry. He was arrested on 7 September.

Tommy Wisbey had been questioned on 20 August and then gone to Spain for a holiday. Apparently he was so confident that he had left no traces he went voluntarily to Scotland Yard on his return. Unfortunately for him, by then police had matched his prints with palm and fingerprints in the bathroom. He was arrested on 11 September.

Welch took a little longer. He had been visited on 14 August as a likely suspect, then interviewed on 16 August. Finally the police got a match of his fingerprints on a can of Pipkin ale. He was arrested on 25 October.

CLOSING IN ON THE REST

Five other people were identified from prints at the farm: Bruce Reynolds's brother-in-law John Daly, Buster Edwards, Roy James, Jimmy White and Bruce Reynolds. All were in hiding or on the move so the police sent out photographs, descriptions and other information to the media and Interpol (see plates 8 and 9).

Goody's photograph and details were not included in the police appeal, but he was under suspicion because of his links to some of the other suspects. However, he had been extremely careful at the farm and left no fingerprint evidence. Even so, as early as 16 August police took a punt and without a warrant searched the house Goody shared with his mother in Putney. Goody was absent.

A few days later a Scotland Yard officer who had been involved in the London airport case received a letter from Goody. (The letter is in the National Archives.) In it, Goody said that despite his acquittal in the London airport case he knew the police still thought he was involved and would, therefore, think he was involved in the train robbery. Since in 1962 it had taken 'eight months and every penny I [he] possessed to fight the charge against me', he intended to lie low until the gang was caught to avoid going through the same ordeal again.

Goody was staying in a room he also had in the Windmill, a pub in Blackfriars where he sometimes helped out behind the bar. On 22 August he borrowed the landlord's car and went up to Leicester to see a beauty-queen girlfriend. He used the landlord's name when he checked into his hotel. According to Fordham, he had to borrow the cash from the beauty queen to pay for the hotel.

On occasion Goody wore glasses. The unlikely consequence of doing so here was that at the hotel he was mistaken for Bruce Reynolds. The receptionist at the Grand in Leicester, having seen Reynolds's photo in the newspaper, phoned the police, who arrested Goody.

When the police searched Goody they found a £5 note and a

10-shilling note. Goody, who had been lent the fiver by his girl-friend, showed his caution and mistrust of the police by asking permission to note down the numbers of the notes — presumably so they couldn't be switched for notes from the robbery. He also had a nice line in slang, referring to the photographs of the wanted men in the newspapers as 'smudges' and calling a police search of someone's place as 'spinning' the place.

His arrest gave the London police the excuse to 'spin' his room at the pub the next day. They took a pair of shoes that they claimed had traces of yellow and khaki paint on them. Such paint had been found at the farm: it had been used to attempt to disguise the lorry and Land Rovers. The pub landlord later testified, on oath, that the shoes were clean when they arrived at the pub. However, when the forensic laboratory had finished its analysis on 13 October, Goody was formally charged and arrested.

The police were tracking everything. They found that one Land Rover had been stolen and the other had been bought by a man answering to Jimmy White's description. Later a witness — Mrs Dalton — reported that two days after the robbery she saw Jimmy White outside Buster Edwards's flat in Twickenham. White moved on to Reigate and then out of reach of the law.

He got away, though his money didn't — a Reigate spending spree did for him. Police had asked shopkeepers to be alert for people flashing large wads of cash. In Reigate, a few days after the robbery, a couple paid for a second-hand caravan on a quiet site with £5 and £1 notes. They gave the name of Ballard and were seen later in the day by the seller of the caravan in a car with a child and a white poodle.

Over the next few days the same woman bought a lot of things for cash in town. The manager of a dress shop sold her a £26 dress and noted the registration number of the car she got into when she left the premises. The car was later stopped. The driver's licence was in the name of James Patton.

Soon after, the police issued photographs of the wanted men and their families. Jimmy White was recognized in Reigate as Ballard/Patton. Police went to the caravan. No one was there, but they found £30,440 hidden behind the panelling in the walls (see plate 10). White's fingerprints were found in the caravan. The police searched White's former house and found banknote wrappers from the robbery. White and his family, however, had disappeared.

Hatherill had set the Fraud Squad on the purchase of Leatherslade Farm. The names of Leonard Field, Brian Field and John Wheater obviously came up. Wheater was interviewed on 19 August. Leonard Field was arrested on 9 September. Brian Field was arrested on 15 September and Wheater was finally arrested on 17 October. All three men were accused of conspiring to rob and obstructing the course of justice.

THE MONEY IN DORKING WOODS

Probably the most mysterious incident in the whole saga of the
Great Train Robbery was the 15 August discovery of £100,900
in four bags in Dorking Woods. The bags were discovered by
chance, and we still don't know why they were left there or who
left them.

A man called Ahern was giving a female work colleague a
lift to their factory in Dorking on his motorbike. Normally they
would be travelling by car, but his car was in for a service.
Because he was travelling by motorcycle he stuck to minor
roads. His engine overheated, so he stopped to let it cool down
in the middle of Dorking Woods. While it did so, Ahern wandered
into the trees.

Ahern's reasons for talking this walk are not known. But it
was fortuitous: Ahern found a leather case, a pigskin holdall
and a zippered plastic bag apparently just dumped. He opened
the plastic bag and found it crammed with £1 notes. He went
back to the road, stopped a car and asked the driver to find a
call box and telephone the police. When the police came they
found a fourth bag. The total amount of money in all four bags
was £100,900.

Stuffed down the lining of one of the bags was a hotel bill from
Bavaria, dated February, in the name of Herr and Frau Field.
The police confronted Brian Field with the bill. He admitted it
was his, but denied the bag belonged to him. He was arrested

and his house searched, though nothing significant was found.

How the money ended up in Dorking Woods has never been satisfactorily explained. Fordham says that anyone could figure out why the money was there and who left it there by looking at the road route to Brighton and reading the shorthand notes of the trial.

Hatherill, writing his memoir six years after Fordham's publication, was not so certain: 'It was never established who dumped these notes, but it seems likely that the money was one of the four shares that I was told were put aside for those who helped the robbers in various ways'. That seems a lot of money just for a helper, but in any case it does not explain how the money ended up in the woods.

ELEVEN DOWN; FIVE TO GO

By now 11 suspects had been charged with five more still to find: John Daly, Buster Edwards, Roy James, Bruce Reynolds and Jimmy White. All those arrested were put on remand in Bedford gaol. Hatherill states that he heard of a plot to rescue Charlie Wilson somewhere between the gaol and Linslade Court, some 20 miles away, on one of his weekly visits. Hatherill foiled the plan by arranging for a section of the women's prison in Aylesbury to be put aside for the robbers.

John Daly, subsequently acquitted, was arrested next, in December 1963. He had been hiding in plain sight in Eaton

Square, dressed in a city suit with bowler and umbrella. He'd grown a beard and lost a lot of weight. The police finally knocked on his door on 3 December, possibly after a tip-off.

Roy James got away with it until 10 December and provided the most thrilling arrest. Hatherill had been alerted to him in August. Police had gone to his flat on 22 August, but he had skipped. Four months later, the police got word that he was living in a mews flat in St John's Wood.

Tommy Butler went there on 10 December. He used an Ordnance Survey map to plot possible escape routes and stationed 30 officers in the immediate vicinity. A policewoman knocked on the front door, pretending to be delivering a parcel. She heard someone moving about inside, but nobody answered the door.

Two other officers clambered over a first floor balcony and smashed a window to get in. As they came in they saw James go out of a skylight onto the roof. They followed him across the rooftops and saw him drop around 30 feet into a garden at the far end of the mews. Unfortunately for him, more policemen had been stationed there.

Before he jumped he dropped down a holdall containing around £12,000. When the police captured him he denied it had anything to do with him. He had a further £130 in an envelope in his pocket. It was his misfortune that two of the £5 notes in the holdall were among the very few whose serial numbers had been recorded. That, combined with fingerprint evidence on a Pyrex dish at the farm, was more than enough to charge him.

According to Hatherill, Tommy Butler was hoping to capture Reynolds that night too as he'd been told the elusive crook would be visiting James. However, Fordham had already debunked this notion in her book seven years earlier, on the grounds that Reynolds and James were not in touch.

Earlier that same evening, another curious incident occurred when Butler's team took an anonymous telephone call telling them to go to a telephone box at Black Horse Court in Southwark where they'd find 'something of interest'.

The 'something of interest' proved to be two potato sacks stuffed with £47,254. Among the money were 57 notes whose serial numbers had been recorded by a bank in Scotland. Why all this cash was left in the phone box has never been satisfactorily explained.

Fordham suggested that, since the phone call coincided with Roy James's arrest, the money was part of James's split, dumped by a friend of his who had panicked.

Hatherill's theory was that the money was part or all of a whack given to a man under suspicion who had been interrogated at length. He was never charged, but Hatherill believes that he got rid of the money because it was getting too hot for him. Frustratingly, the files at the National Archives have no record of this interrogation.

The other theory is that the money was intended to be a

'bung' for a crooked policeman, but the deal went awry.

On 16 August Bruce Reynolds had left the newly-purchased Austin Healey at a garage in Hayes, Middlesex. He never went back for it. On 23 August police had raided his second home in Putney, but they had missed him.

In his autobiography, Reynolds says he and his wife and child first stayed with an old friend in Queensway, but that they were nervous because a big reward had been announced. Reynolds also says that he heard much later that he was linked to the train robbery because Detective Chief Superintendent Ernie Millen, operational head of the Flying Squad, and his boss, George Hatherill, visited an informant in prison who confirmed the names already on their 'hit list'.

When the newspapers named Jimmy White, Reynolds assumed someone had grassed, because there was no other reason for White to be a suspect. His relationship with the others was not known: he had been on the run for years and was careful not to attract attention. Except for when his wife went on a shopping spree, of course.

Reynolds and his wife then hid for six months in a house he'd bought in Albert Mews, Kensington. He later wrote that he watched what was going on with 'disbelief at some of the revelations emerging from the Yard'.

Knowing how the relationship between some police officers and criminals worked, Reynolds expected 'irregularities'. This time, he felt it was different. 'The Flying Squad was determined that nobody slipped through the net — not even the innocent.'

Ironically, Reynolds, the lover of fine cuisine and expensive holidays in the south of France, had been identified by a partial print on a ketchup bottle at the farm. According to Reynolds, Detective Superintendent Maurice Ray, the fingerprints expert, was a drinking acquaintance from the Marlborough pub. As fellow regulars, Reynolds said, 'we had enjoyed the not irregular after-hours piss-ups'. Whether he was saying this to muddy the waters about police/criminal collusion it is hard to say. He was writing in 1995, when it was taken for granted that the lives of cops and robbers often overlapped.

Whilst the Reynolds were moving from London flat to London flat, they were actually burgled. This could have been coincidence, but more likely it was a demonstration that there is in fact no 'honour among thieves'. In subsequent months, usually when the robbers were most vulnerable, other villains were quick to get a piece of that massive take.

A neighbour saw the burglary and called the police. When the police came round, Reynolds stripped off and jumped into bed. His wife headed the police off by saying she was a married woman and this man was her lover, visiting in her husband's absence. The police took a (false) name from Reynolds then politely withdrew.

When, in a matter of hours, the name proved to be false, the police returned in force, but the Reynolds were gone.

GOING TO TRIAL

By December, nine of the men who had been on the track were in custody. Three, who the police were actively looking for, were still on the run: Jimmy White, Bruce Reynolds and Buster Edwards. Accomplices brought the number of people in custody to 19. The police decided to proceed against them.

The trial began at Aylesbury under Mr (later Lord) Edmund Justice Davies on 20 January 1964. It lasted until 17 April, becoming in the process the longest trial in British criminal history up to that time. The 19 defendants included relatives and associates of the men who had actually been on the track.

There was a small army of witnesses — 209 of them — and vast swathes of documentation. The National Archives' court records are in a series of files that placed side by side would probably extend to around 8 feet in length. There were 618 exhibits (though over 1,000 were prepared, see plates 15 and 16). The list of exhibits included: Playing board (Monopoly); 16 Chance cards; 15 Community Chest cards; 27 title deed cards; 13 imitation notes; a dice; 12 houses; 4 hotels. (ASSI 13/643)

The Crown was unable to produce a single witness to identify any of the accused as being present on the track. Roger Cordrey had pleaded guilty — though without implicating anyone else — and he and seven others (the ones accused of receiving) were set down for a later date.

There had been talk of moving the trial to the Old Bailey, but the decision was taken to transform Aylesbury's District Council offices into a courtroom as the Assize Court was too small to hold so many people. The prosecution stayed at The Bell at Aston Clifton, a pub run by an ex-solicitor with a reputation for a good wine cellar. The press hung out at the Bull's Head in Aylesbury's central square.

On the 17th day of the trial, Tuesday 11 February, John Daly was acquitted. The day before, the prosecution had completed outlining its case and the defence had, as a formality, submitted 'No case to answer' for all the defendants. The judge allowed Daly's submission. The only evidence against Daly was his fingerprints on a set of Monopoly tokens. The judge stated that their discovery 'implied no more than suspicion against him' since the prints could have got on the set at any time and did not prove he had been at the farm.

The defence began on Friday 14 February. The main problem for the defendants was explaining how their fingerprints came to be found at Leatherslade Farm. Each defendant came up with an ingenious excuse. Any one of these might have been plausible. Put together, they sounded less convincing.

For example, Jim Hussey stated that 'Dark Ronnie', a friend called Ronnie Dark, wanted his help to deliver some groceries on Saturday 10 August. As this friend turned up in a lorry, so too did Bob Welch and Tommy Wisbey to see if Hussey wanted to go out for a drink. Hussey decided he could not help with the errand as he had to look after his mother, but Welch and Wisbey volunteered. All this was decided in the street, where Hussey lifted the tarpaulin of the lorry and took an apple. That, he said, is why his prints were on the tail board of the lorry.

Welch and Wisbey went with Dark Ronnie down to a place that turned out to be Leatherslade Farm. Whilst there Wisbey washed his hands in the bathroom and left fingerprints on the towel rail. Welch, meanwhile, a former licensee, picked up a can of Pipkins ale for the reason that he was 'interested in these new cans'.

Ronnie Dark was not immediately produced in court, but he did testify, nervously, on the 23rd day of the trial after ads had been put in the press to find him. He corroborated the unlikely story, but he proved a jittery witness and neither judge nor jury were convinced by his testimony.

Roy James chose not to go into the witness box in his own defence. Charlie Wilson took the same decision. One problem for Wilson was Tommy Butler's claim about the poppy quote made by Wilson (see p. 64).

This remark had been widely reported in the press so that, although Wilson's barrister got it excluded at the trial, the damage had been done.

GOODY TAKES THE STAND

Goody did take the stand. The only evidence against him was the paint on the soles of his shoes. Unfortunately for him, by sticking to his alibi of being on an Irish holiday, which he said was paid for by the profits of a smuggling racket, he allowed the prosecution to refer to his criminal record. This included the London airport job for which he had been twice tried and then finally acquitted.

With hindsight it seems quite possible that Goody was 'fitted up' by the police with the paint on the soles of his shoes as he had been scrupulously careful at the farm. His defence pointed out that a Detective Constable Milner had seen a squashed tin of paint at Leatherslade Farm on 14 August. Tommy Butler and Chief Inspector Vibart were at the farm on 19 August. But nobody seemed to care about the squashed tin of paint until 28 August, when Milner collected it. (Dr Holden, the analyst, received it on 29 August.) The defence more or less wondered whether the sudden interest was because the police had located Goody on his trip to Leicester on 22 August, but had so far found no evidence against him. Furthermore, Milner in his evidence stated that he thought the police guard on the farm had been lifted on 26 August. Consequently, the tin of paint was left unattended for a further two days until 28 August.

Goody's defence counsel also made much of the illegal search of the house Goody shared with his mother in Putney a week before he was detained in Leicester. The search had been carried out by Detective Sergeant John Swain. He claimed to have forgotten that no warrant to search the premises had been made out when he went to Putney. The judge was incredulous at this forgetfulness and Swain was given a hard time.

The following exchange occurred between Swain and Goody's counsel after Swain admitted he had told Goody's mother that he did have a warrant (J 82/427/5B 808):

> Counsel: Do you mean you told her a lie?
>
> Swain: It was a mistake ... I had other warrants to search other addresses and I was also told to search that address. I did not have a warrant ... If she had not allowed us to go in we would have got a warrant.
>
> Counsel: If you told her you had a warrant she could not refuse you.
>
> Swain: She could have asked to see it but it did not arise.

When the police took the pair of shoes (brown suede) from the Windmill pub they also took a British passport. A little later in this section of the trial (and in file J 82/427/5B 808) the judge, referring to this passport, revealed himself to be almost the typical caricature of the querulous English judge. The passport had been passed to the jury.

> Judge Davies: If you compare the photograph with the gentleman who is second from the left on the back row of the accused, you may or may not see some similarity.
>
> Mr Speed: Your Lordship said second from the left. It is in fact the third.
>
> Davies: The third from the left. The officer there obscured him. I had not seen the gentleman who is first in the back row

throughout this trial at any stage … Now I do see him. I cannot see him from where I am at all.

At the trial, during his summation (J 82/440), the judge said:

Mr Goody is obviously a live and energetic man, about the 30 mark, a man of 6ft or more, and he has exhibited, you may think, in that witness box, a sharp and lively intelligence and has manifested an extremely strong and dynamic personality.

There is no fingerprint evidence in relation to him at all. His clothing … no sign of paint … No stolen money traced to him … at least two identity parades and no one picked him out.

It was the paint on the shoes.

The prosecution was able to use Goody's previous record against him because of his alibi. By contrast, Ronnie Biggs's trial was halted because a police witness, Inspector Morris of the Surrey Constabulary, made reference to the thief's previous record. Morris mentioned that Biggs had met Bruce Reynolds in prison. Without explaining why, the judge had the jury removed and then discussed with Biggs's council—Peta Fordham's husband, in fact—what to do about the policeman's 'grossly improper' reference to Biggs's imprisonment. It was agreed that Biggs would be sent back to prison and await a new trial whilst this trial continued without him.

12 Chief Superintendent Tommy Butler in 1969, when Bruce Reynolds was tried and convicted. Butler died the next year.

13 *Right:* The police exhibits room. Items displayed include the famous Monopoly board, which for many symbolized the playful side of the crime. (HO 242/2)

14 *Below:* The Buckinghamshire police incident room from which the case was investigated. (HO 242/2)

R. *v.* CORDERY AND OTHERS

LIST OF EXHIBITS.

Number or other identifying mark on Exhibit.	Short description of Exhibit.	Produced by Prosecution or Defence.	Name and Address of Person retaining Exhibit.	Directions of the Judge of the Court of Trial.
1	Plan of detached train unit	Prosecution		
2	Plan of diesel engine	do		
3	Plan of sorting van	do		
4	Plan of Leatherslade Farmhouse	do		
5	Plan of Leatherslade Farm	do		
6	Plan of mid-Buckinghamshire	do		
7	Plan of Royal Mail Train	do		
8	Flex	do		
9	Plan of railway track	do		
10	Album of 27 photographs	do		
11	Album of 13 photographs	do		
12	Johnsons Travelkit	do		
13	Helmet	do		
14	Boiler suit	do		
15	Handcuffs	do		
16	Overalls	do		
17	Jacket	do		
18	Jacket	do		
19	Marker	do		
20	Axe	do		
21	Stocking	do		
22	£7.10s.0d. in notes	do		

PLAN OF LEATHERSLADE FARM HOUSE OAKLEY

15 *Left:* The police prepared over 1,000 exhibits, 618 of which were presented in court; this is the first page of the list. (ASSI 13/643)

16 *Right:* Plan of Leatherslade Farm produced as a police exhibit. (ASSI 13/659)

both the first and second counts. You are the only one
out of the accused in respect of whom it has been proved that
you actually received a substantial part of the stolen
moneys. On your arrest you still had in your possession
over £12,000 which I have no doubt was the result of exchange
out of the original stolen moneys received by you. I
entertain no doubt that the original sum you received
substantially exceeded that figure. Your record in the
past is a bad one and corrective training seems to have done
you little or no good. Yet you have ability of a kind which
would have assured you an honest livelihood of substantial
proportions; for in a very short space of time you had, as your
learned counsel has said, brilliant and meteoric success as
a racing driver. I strongly suspect that it was your
known talent as a driver which enabled you to play an important
part in the perpetration of this grave crime. It may be,
as you say, that you personally have never resorted to physical
violence, but you nevertheless stand convicted of participating
with others in armed robbery and for that you must be sentenced.
You have told me that you went to Leatherslade Farm knowing you
were doing wrong, that you became involved, but not in the
robbery, and then ran away. I do not find it possible to
differentiate your case from that of most of the other accused.
You will accordingly go to prison for concurrent terms of
25 years on the first count and 30 years on the second count.

(The Accused Roy John James left the dock).

THE ASSISTANT CLERK OF ASSIZE: Put up Douglas Gordon Goody.

MR. JUSTICE DAVIES: Douglas Gordon Goody, you have been convicted
on the first and second counts of this indictment. You have
a bad record, notably with a conviction for grave violence
at the early age of 18 and you qualify for preventive detention.
Yet, in some respects, you present to this court one of the
saddest problems by which it is confronted in this trial. You
have manifest gifts of personality and intelligence which
might have carried you far had they been directed to honesty.
I have not seen you in court for the best part of three
months without noticing signs that you are a man capable of
inspiring the admiration of your fellow accused. In the
Army you earned a very good character assessment and it is
easy to imagine you becoming, in an entirely honourable role,
a leader of your comrades, but you have become a dangerous
menace to society.

The Crown have said that they do not consider this
criminal enterprise was the product of any criminal master
mind. I do not know that I necessarily agree with the Crown
in this respect. I strongly suspect that you played a major
role, both in the conspiracy and   in the actual robbery.
Suspicion, however, is not good enough for me any more than
it would be for a jury. It would be, therefore, quite
wrong for me to cause my suspicions to lead to imposing upon
you any heavier sentence than upon other accused and I shall
not do so. You will go to prison for concurrent terms of
25 years on the first count and 30 years on the second count.

(The Accused Douglas Gordon Goody left the dock).

THE ASSISTANT CLERK OF ASSIZE: Put up Brian Arthur Field.

MR. JUSTICE DAVIES: Brian Arthur Field, you have been convicted
under count 1 and count 12 of conspiracy to rob the mail
and of conspiracy to obstruct the course of justice. Of the
righteousness of both verdicts I personally entertain no
doubt whatsoever. You had earned an excellent reputation
beginning with little original advantages. By a combination
of native ability of no mean kind and hard work you had

68.

17 *Left:* A page from Mr Justice Edmund Davies's summing up, which provides interesting character sketches of the robbers. Here he deals with Roy James, Gordon Goody and Brian Field. (ASSI 13/764)

18 *Above:* The *Daily Mirror* on 16 April 1964, the day after the main group of robbers was sentenced to a total of 307 years' imprisonment.

BIGGS

Ronald, Arthur.

born on 8th August 1929 in BRIXTON/LONDON (Great Britain)
son of BIGGS given name not known
married to Renée ?
OCCUPATION : builder
NATIONALITY : British
IDENTITY HAS BEEN CHECKED AND IS CORRECT
DESCRIPTION : see photo and fingerprints, height 6'1", grey eyes, dark brown curly hair.
Scar on left wrist; long fingers.

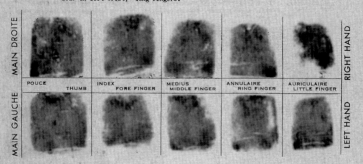

	POUCE THUMB	INDEX FORE FINGER	MEDIUS MIDDLE FINGER	ANNULAIRE RING FINGER	AURICULAIRE LITTLE FINGER	

MAIN DROITE — RIGHT HAND

MAIN GAUCHE — LEFT HAND

FINGERPRINTED AND PHOTOGRAPHED IN LONDON (Great Britain) in 1963

PREVIOUS CONVICTIONS :
This man has a long criminal record in GREAT
BRITAIN : convicted five times for robbery; twice
for receiving; twice for taking and driving away motor
vehicles without the consent of the owner; seven times
for breaking and entering and burglary; etc.---
After the GLASGOW-LONDON mail train robbery on 8/8/1963,
he was sentenced to 30 years' imprisonment; he escaped
from WANDSWORTH prison in London on 8/7/1965 with three
other prisoners.

MISCELLANEOUS INFORMATION :
Was accompanied by : his wife; Robert Alves Anderson; Eric Flower; Patrick Doyle; Paul
Seabourne; Francis Victor Hornett.-- Could be in the company of other members of the gang which
robbed the mail train at Cheddington on 8/8/1963, are at large and are the subjects of the following
I.C.P.O.-INTERPOL international notices : EDWARDS Ronald, notice 555/63 A 4786 of September 1963;
REYNOLDS Bruce Richard, n°550/63 A 4782 of September 1963; WHITE James Edward, n°551/63 A 4783 of
September 1963; WILSON Charles, Frederick, n°517/64 A 5167 of November 1964.---- A warrant of arrest
will be issued shortly.---- EXTRADITION WILL BE REQUESTED.

REASON FOR THIS CIRCULATION :
Done at the request of the BRITISH authorities in order to discover his whereabouts. If found
please detain and inform immediately : The British Representative, International Criminal Police
Organization, National Office, Criminal Investigation Department, New Scotland Yard, LONDON SW 1
(INTERPOL LONDON SW 1), and also : the I.C.P.O.-INTERPOL, General Secretariat, 37 bis rue Paul Valé-
ry. PARIS (INTERPOL PARIS).

I.C.P.O. PARIS
August 1965

File N° : 387/65
Control N° : A. 5408

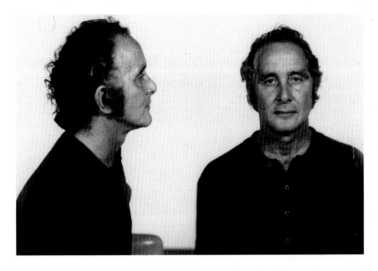

19 *Left:* Interpol notice for Ronnie Biggs (his fingerprints blurred here for Data Protection purposes) after his 1965 prison escape. (FCO 53/400)

20 *Above:* Police photograph of Ronnie Biggs used by the Foreign Office in their dealings with Brazil in the 1970s. (FCO 53/401)

Train Robbers' Sentences

1. Lord Stonham saw Mr. Wilfrid Fordham, Q.C., at 5.15 p.m. on 12th June. Mr. Fordham apologised for the absence of Mr. John Mathew who was unfortunately prevented from accompanying him but who would certainly like to be present when the Home Secretary was able to see them.

2. Mr. Fordham said that Mr. Justice Shaw who had submitted and largely prepared the original memorandum before his promotion to the Bench could not now for obvious reasons pursue the matter, but had authorised him to say that he still fully supported the application. A draft of the memorandum had also been shown to Lord Justice Edmund Davies, who had imposed the 30 years' sentence and who was much disturbed about the present position.

3. Mr. Fordham said that after the original trial and appeal, counsel accepted that nothing more could and should be done to challenge further the very long sentences imposed. The substantially shorter sentences later passed on White and Edwardes had, however, materially altered the situation. He could say in confidence that this wide disparity had caused great bitterness among the other prisoners. His wife, who was a journalist (Crime Consultant to the 'Sunday Times'), had made a special study of the case and had written a book about it, and she had since kept in touch with Goody. She was fully satisfied that the only member of the gang who had used violence, that is to say, the man who struck down the train driver, was Edwardes. This was known to all the convicted men, though none of them say so; it was not known to all Mr. Fordham's colleagues at the Bar. A person who had been acquitted in the case [? Daly] had given his wife the fullest possible information.

4. Mr. Fordham said that his wife had/confidential correspondence with Lord Justice Edmund Davies, and he then read his wife's letter to the Judge. This described her dealings with Goody and enlarged on his qualities. It repeated that the crime had been planned as a non-violent one, and alleged that persons outside prison had by now embezzled (sic) all the stolen money. Mr. Fordham added that, as the governor of Parkhurst prison could confirm, the prisoners there were behaving admirably under difficult conditions, and he was sure that Goody would be the last man to try to escape.

5. Reverting to the question of the disparity of the sentences, Mr. Fordham said that he and his colleagues at the Bar were concerned that justice should be seen to be equal. Mr. Justice Edmund Davies (as he then was) had made it clear at the trial that all those convicted of robbery had to be dealt with in the same way,

1.

... Mr. Fordham himself) and Edwardes ... mitigating circumstances on behalf ... al justification for the difference ... gned the memorandum felt that ... be given the opportunity to ... or that in some way some ... risoners that they would be ... ole or that their sentences

... t the Home Secretary naturally ... f counsel in this matter and ... very carefully. Having regard ... onsibility for public order, ... im to take action which would ... ly severe sentences designed ... rime, and his conclusion was ... him to use his powers under ... 1907 to refer the case back ... went on to explain in detail ... he lines set out in the

... nham explained that all the ... become eligible for ... had served one-third of ... e so considered, though it ... e decision would be. ... ere not aware that they ... in due course and at his ... r whether anything further ... ssure them on this point. ... he would convey to the ... . Fordham had made to him, ... tten note of the detailed ... conclude that he could ... by counsel.

21 Home Office correspondence documenting the involvement in the case of the journalist Peta Fordham, who was particularly concerned with the welfare of Gordon Goody. (HO 291/929)

THE VERDICTS ARE IN

The summing up began eight weeks after the opening of the case (J 82, various). It lasted six days. The jury left the court at 3.36 pm on Monday 23 March. They reached a verdict on Wednesday 25 March at 8.15 pm. The next morning the court convened at 10.30 am.

All the accused were found guilty on all charges, with the exception of Brian Field and Leonard Field (who were found guilty of conspiracy and obstructing the course of justice but not guilty of robbing or receiving).

The judge thanked the jurors, joking to the foreman: 'You and I have been sitting in this Court for so long that, to quote another judge on another occasion, "Life will never seem quite the same without you".'

Although the verdicts had been given, the sentences were postponed until the trial of Ronnie Biggs and the defence speeches in mitigation.

The trial of Ronnie Biggs opened on Wednesday 8 April. It took only five days. He was found guilty. The accomplices charged with receiving stolen money—five men and one woman—then appeared. The woman and one man were discharged. Two were given conditional discharges; a fourth, who had pleaded guilty to receiving £2,000, got three years; and a man who pleaded guilty to receiving £518, was sentenced to one year.

On Thursday 16 April all the convicted prisoners came back to court to be sentenced. Roger Cordrey was the first to be sentenced 'out of certainly eleven greedy men whom hope of gain allured'. A hint of what was coming came in the judge's next remark (J 82/439):

> You and your co-accused have been convicted of complicity, in one way or another, of a crime which in its impudence and enormity is the first of its kind in this country. I propose to do all within my power to ensure it will be the last of its kind; for your outrageous conduct constitutes an intolerable menace to the well-being of society.

Judge Davies dismissed 'any romantic notions of dare devilry'. 'This,' he said, 'is nothing more than a sordid crime of violence inspired by vast greed.' To deal with it leniently would be 'a positively evil thing'.

> When grave crime is committed it calls for grave punishment, not for the purpose of mere retribution but so that others similarly tempted shall be brought to the sharp realization that crime does not pay....

The judge referred to the violence inflicted on driver Jack Mills, who had testified in court in a quiet voice.

> As to violence, anybody who has seen that nerve-shattered engine driver can have no doubt of the terrifying effect on law-abiding citizens of a concerted assault by masked and armed robbers in lonely darkness.

The judge's view was that criminals should be aware 'the higher the prize ... the punishment they risk will be proportionately greater'.

Cordrey had pleaded guilty and helped the police recover almost £140,000. The judge had made it clear that since it was 'impossible to determine exactly what part was played by each of the eleven accused convicted of the larger conspiracy or the eight convicted of the actual robbery', the robbers were all going to be 'treated in the same manner'—with the exception of Cordrey and Bill Boal.

Bill Boal, very small beer, almost certainly not involved in the robbery except after the fact, suffered from his connection to Cordrey, who had pleaded guilty, and the fact that all the other accused were sticking to not-guilty stories so could not say he hadn't been with them. He was extended 'some measure of mercy' on the grounds of his age (he was 50) and because the judge couldn't believe he 'was one of the originators of the conspiracy or that you played a very dynamic part in it or of the robbery itself'.

The judge sentenced Cordrey to 20 years and his mercy to Boal took the form of concurrent sentences of 21 and 24 years.

Charlie Wilson was next. 'No one has said less than you throughout this long trial,' the judge said. 'Indeed, I doubt if you have spoken half a dozen words. Certainly no word of repentance has been expressed by you.' The judge sentenced him to 30 years.

Biggs followed. While the judge agreed that he 'had no special talent' and was 'plainly not an originator of the conspiracy', he did regard him as 'a specious and facile liar'. However, 'I add not a day to your sentence on that account'. Biggs got 30 years.

And so it went on: Thomas William Wisbey; Robert Alfred Welch; James Hussey; Roy John James; and Douglas Gordon Goody each got 30 years (see plate 17). Brian Arthur Field and Leonard Dennis Field each got 25 years. John Wheater, dragged into it—almost certainly unwittingly—by his clerk, Brian Field, got three years.

There was absolutely no evidence connecting any of the accused to the actual scene of the crime. And even at the farm, most of the prints were on objects that hadn't always been at the farm so could, conceivably, have been handled elsewhere. (The judge recognized this in John Daly's case.)

Everyone in court was shocked by the severity of the main sentences—as were those robbers still on the run.

The appeals were heard in August 1964. Mr Justice Fenton Atkinson of the Court of Criminal Appeal described the robbery as 'organised banditry', an 'act of warfare against the community' and dismissed all but four of the appeals.

He made exceptions of Brian Field, Roger Cordrey and Bill Boal. The fact that Brian Field had been found not guilty of either taking part in the robbery or receiving stolen money left no grounds for finding him guilty of conspiracy to rob. His sentence of 25 years was quashed, leaving him with just a five-year sentence for obstruction of justice. When he got out he pretty much disappeared from public view.

The court of appeal accepted that Boal probably wasn't involved in the robbery so substituted for the original charges one of receiving stolen money. It did the same for Roger Cordrey. However, the two men still got hefty sentences for that: 14 years each.

ESCAPE!

Charlie Wilson, imprisoned in Winson Green, Birmingham, did not attend his appeal at the Law Courts in London. Instead, on the night of 12 August 1964, men scaled the Victorian prison's outer walls with ladders, somehow got through locked doors, gagged and bound a prison warden and freed Wilson. Locking doors after them, they left with him. Wilson, his wife and two children disappeared.

This dramatic escape fed into the public fascination with the daredevil robbery. Almost a year later, on 8 July 1965, another train robber escaped from a different prison. Ronnie Biggs might have been a minor member of the robbery gang but someone thought him worth springing. He was in Wandsworth, another Victorian prison.

Hatherill in his memoirs believed that Briggs was sprung thanks to his childhood friend, Eric Flowers, who was also incarcerated in Wandsworth. However, Hatherill tells a confusing story in which Flowers plans it on his own release yet is still in prison when the break happens, and joins Biggs in his escape up a ladder. According to Biggs, writing in the *Sun* in the late sixties, a friend he calls Paul Seabourne planned the escape.

What is known for certain is that an old furniture van was parked one afternoon alongside a deserted part of the prison wall. There was a hole in the roof and a kind of lift inside it. When Biggs came out into the exercise yard two masked men came out of the van on the end of the lift and lowered a flexible ladder down 25 feet into the exercise yard. Biggs, Flowers and two other men climbed out, jumped down through the hole in the van's roof, landed on a mattress, then transferred to a waiting car and drove off.

There were seven men involved, and all but Biggs and Flowers were quickly traced and arrested. Freddie Foreman apparently provided a safe house for Biggs. In the *Sun* Biggs said that he and Flowers were smuggled to France by a man called George for plastic surgery. Before long, however, he and his wife Charmian were in Australia under false names.

REYNOLDS, EDWARDS, WHITE AND WILSON

Bruce Reynolds, Buster Edwards and Jimmy White were in hiding when the imprisoned robbers appealed against their lengthy sentences. When the appeals were turned down they had no incentive to turn themselves in.

Bruce Reynolds and Buster Edwards decided to go abroad. Reynolds went to the south of France and his wife went to see Tommy Butler who questioned her then let her go. She got a passport in the name of Angela Green and by October had joined Bruce in the south of France. By Christmas, however, they were in Mexico City and Buster and his wife had joined them.

By early 1966 White had decided to give himself up. He had lost much of his share of the loot at the caravan and life on the run was expensive, especially when other crooks were nibbling away at what money he did have. He never gave a reason for giving himself up. He did find £7,000 to give to the police. He pleaded guilty, of course, but didn't give anyone else up. At his trial in June 1966 he received 18 years, implicit acknowledgement by the judiciary that the original sentences had been unduly harsh.

Reynolds persuaded Buster Edwards and his wife to go to Mexico City, but they were miserable there, disliking the heat, the food and the drink. Piers Paul Read believed that Edwards had wanted to give himself up almost from the off—and that the money found in the telephone box on the night of Roy James's capture was somehow linked to a deal Edwards was trying to make to get a reduced sentence.

Edwards returned to England. Freddie Foreman claimed

that in 1966 he arranged a deal for Edwards to give himself up on 19 September in exchange for a reduced sentence. However, Hatherill's account has Tommy Butler tracing and arresting him, thanks to fingerprints found on a car used by a business firm he was connected with. Edwards had no money to give back. He was tried and convicted in December 1966 and sentenced to 15 years.

Charlie Wilson had started a new life in a small town in Quebec. Butler tracked him down there and in 1967 turned up on Wilson's doorstep accompanied by a posse of Mounties and arrested him.

FINALLY — BRUCE REYNOLDS CAUGHT

Reynolds was on the loose for over five years. According to later police investigations, between June 1964 and August 1967 he travelled to France, Belgium, Germany, Mexico, Canada and the USA. He lived in the South of France, Mexico and the USA. He maintained bank accounts in Mexico and Canada. Eventually, homesick and running short of money — he'd been living high on the hog whilst on the run — he returned to Britain and rented a villa in Torquay (19 Braddons Hill Road East) in the name of Hiller.

He'd been there around two months when, on 8 November 1968 at 6.30 am, Tommy Butler turned up on the doorstep to arrest him. Butler had been due to retire the year before, but had asked to stay on to catch the rest of the Great Train Robbers.

According to Butler's police report (quoted in court in ASSI 13/651A) he found Reynolds in bed and Reynolds said: 'Well, this is it I suppose. I'm glad it's all over. It's no life for anyone, always drifting about.' As he was getting dressed, he went on: "I had been thinking for some time of giving myself up, you know, but this mastermind business the newspapers made a lot of fuss about just isn't true."

Among his possessions were passports in the names of Keith Clement Miller, George Firth and Terence Overton. His wife had three passports in the names Angela Green, Pauline Firth and Joyce Overton.

When Butler told Reynolds at the police station that they knew he'd purchased at least five 'good quality' motor cars, Reynolds is said to have shrugged and said "*c'est la vie*", though using the French phrase perhaps to say "that's the life" rather than the more usual "that's life". Other accounts have him saying it when Butler arrested him at the villa in Torquay.

Reynolds had been worried that if the press speculation that he was the mastermind behind the Robbery was shown to be true he would get a heavier sentence than his co-conspirators, so he was quick to distance himself from such ideas. He also offered £6,000 as restitution.

When Bruce Reynolds went on trial, in January 1969, at Buckingham Assizes, in Aylesbury, the judge, Mr Justice

Thomson, asked Tommy Butler what position the robber held in the gang's hierarchy. The policeman replied: 'Somewhere near the top.'

Reynolds asked his lawyer, Cyril Salmon, to thank Tommy Butler in open court for the 'kindness and courtesy' he had extended to his wife and children. However, in his autobiography Reynolds comments that in hunting down the other robbers, Butler 'did what he had to do'. (There is absolutely no proof that Butler cut any corners in his investigation of the robbery.)

Reynold's counsel was complimented on his plea of mitigation for the robber by the judge. However, on 14 January 1969 the judge concluded:

> The fact that you avoided arrest for five years and, presumably, during that time were able to enjoy the fruits of your crime, does not, in my view, constitute any reason for passing upon you any less sentence than you would have received then, even though it is no doubt true that your enjoyment of these fruits was associated with the fear of ultimate arrest.

Reynolds received 25 years. The longest he had been in prison before this was around three-and-a-half years.

CRITICISM OF THE POLICE

Perhaps surprisingly, given they had virtually the whole gang behind bars within six months, the police were criticized for the way they had handled the investigation of the Great Train Robbery. An official report by E.J. Dodd in 1965 (HO 242/4) listed some errors that John Cheney, the Chief Constable of Buckinghamshire, accepted.

There was certainly one blunder, though it had no bad consequences. The clothes worn by Mills were not taken for blood samples until 12 August. 'Valuable evidence could have been destroyed', the report commented. And by January 1965 the total amount of money recovered was only £335, 518.

In a note in the Archive (H 242/3), a Home Office official joked to Peter Brodie of HM Inspector of Constabulary about Cheney's acceptance:

> Dear Peter, you will be interested to see John Cheney's reaction to the report on the Great Train Robbery. I am very glad that he did not take offence at any of the rather subtly concealed criticisms of his force. No doubt the subsequent dinner with Elizabeth Taylor and Richard Burton at the Dorchester served to heal any wounds that may have been left after reading the report.

There are no more details of this dinner with the Angelina Jolie and Brad Pitt of their day — *Cleopatra*, the turgid film on which

they met, had come out in the summer of 1963 — although the
same Home Office official also wrote impishly to Cheney:

> I thought you looked very perky last Saturday at the Trooping
> and now I realise the reason. Dinner with Elizabeth Taylor,
> even if accompanied by her husband, must be quite some-
> thing…

CHAPTER FIVE

The Crooks' Fates

The unhappy Bill Boal died in prison, leaving a wife and children behind. John Wheater and Brian Field were the first to be released and both disappeared from public view.

There had been much talk of the severity of the original sentences at the time in the press and even in Parliament. Nothing was done until the shorter sentences for Jimmy White and Buster Edwards indicated that the judiciary implicitly recognized the harshness of the original judge.

Seven of the robbers were paroled in August 1975, having served just over 10 years of their 30-year sentences. That left Charlie Wilson and Bruce Reynolds inside, with Ronnie Biggs on the loose. First these seven, with the tacit approval of the other three, sold their imaginative version of events to W.H. Allen to be turned into Piers Paul Read's *The Robbers*. Then they went their separate ways.

On his release Roger Cordrey went back to his former profession of florist. Jimmy White ran a painting and decorating business. Bobby Welch ran a gambling club. In prison he'd had a cartilage operation that had gone wrong and could now walk only with the aid of crutches.

Tommy Wisbey bought a pub and Jim Hussey opened a car dealership in Warren Street. However, in the early nineties Wisbey and Hussey were again in prison, this time on cocaine-trafficking charges.

Gordon Goody had spent some time at Parkhurst and had written a long, cogent letter about conditions there in an impressive italic script (PDG 196/19/1). In the letter he had noted: 'The shock of my sentence was so great that for many months I gave serious thought to ending my life. Everything looked so utterly hopeless for me.'

Peta Fordham, via her husband, the barrister Wilfrid Fordham, had been energetic in her attempts to get Goody's sentence reduced. In the Home Office correspondence already quoted (HO 291/929, see plate 21), a clerk noted:

> Mr Fordham said that his wife had confidential correspondence with Lord Justice Edmund Davies [the judge at the original trial] and he then read his wife's letter to the Judge. This described her dealings with Goody and enlarged on his qualities ... Mr Fordham added that, as the governor of Parkhurst prison could confirm, the [Great Train Robbery] prisoners there were behaving admirably under difficult conditions, and he was sure that Goody would be the last man to try to escape.

When Goody was released from prison in 1975 he moved back into wholesale fruit and vegetables. He later bought property and a bar in Spain, where he lived quietly thereafter.

After his release from Pentonville on 15 September 1978 Charlie Wilson laid low, working on a fruit and veg stall belonging to an old friend and living in a small flat in Twickenham. Then in March 1980 he was ordered to pay income tax on £30,000 his wife, Pat, had earned 12 years earlier from newspaper articles she had written about the robbery and their life on the run. According to Wensley Clarkson in *Killing Charlie*, 'Charlie saw this as yet more evidence that the Establishment was still after him.'

Wilson then went into business with Roy James on a classic 'long firm' scam. James had come out of prison in 1975 and tried to get back into motor racing. Within a month he'd broken his leg test-racing at Silverstone. His motor racing career over, he focused on his Hatton Garden silversmithing and this work with Wilson on the side.

According to Clarkson the two men imported over 76,000 Maple Leaf gold coins and Krugerrands into the UK. The coins were VAT-exempt. They were then melted down and the gold sold with VAT added on. The classic long-firm sting was then to disappear, pocketing the 15 per cent VAT due to Customs and Excise. Clarkson reckons Wilson and James bought and melted down £16 million worth of gold coins and Krugerrands.

How they funded this is not clear, but perhaps both men still had money from the Great Train Robbery at their disposal. Operating at that sort of level, however, was bound to attract attention. On 4 April 1983 Wilson was arrested and he, James and six others were remanded in custody to face a charge of conspiring to defraud Customs and Excise. Eventually James was acquitted and Wilson agreed to pay £400,000 to Customs to avoid a retrial.

The two men went their separate ways, but Wilson was under arrest again in October 1984 for plotting a robbery and possessing two sawn-off shotguns. However, the case was thrown out of court because of 'disquieting features'—the disquiet was caused by the fact that the charge was clearly a 'fit-up' by two corrupt policemen.

Wilson had bought a small apartment near Marbella on the Costa del Sol and he and his wife, Pat, now moved there full-time. Spain was a haven for British criminals as there had been no extradition treaty between the two countries since 1978, but at the time Wilson was not actually wanted for anything.

Spain was the route into Europe for South American cocaine and North African cannabis. Clarkson goes into some detail in his book about how British villains were heavily involved with the drugs trade. He suggests that Wilson was part of it, even visiting Colombia to talk with the ruthless Medellin drug cartel. The Spanish police, British police and British Customs and Excise were all convinced that Wilson was involved in drug smuggling.

On 23 April 1990 Charlie Wilson and his wife, Pat, were at their villa in Marbella. It was their 35th wedding anniversary.

Late in the afternoon, Pat answered the door to a young Londoner in a grey tracksuit and baseball cap. He asked for Wilson.

Wilson invited him in and the two men walked out onto the terrace where they stood talking for a few minutes. Pat, elsewhere in the house, heard raised voices then two loud bangs.

Wilson, who had developed emphysema in recent years, had been kicked between the legs then had his nose broken by a punch to the face. A bullet to the neck severed his carotid artery. A second bullet entered his mouth and exited out of the back of his head. Then the young man, a professional hit man, went over the back wall.

Wilson was buried in Streatham cemetery on 10 May 1990. There were five limousines in a convoy of fifty cars. On the roof rack of the first car a floral display picked out the name 'Chas'. As part of the funeral service, Wilson's signature tune was played: 'My Way'. Reynolds, in military mode again, says that his epitaph for Wilson was simply: 'He never left anyone behind.' No one has ever been convicted of Wilson's murder.

After Roy James had been acquitted in 1983 of the VAT scam he and Wilson had carried out, he seemed to go straight, focusing on his work as a silversmith. A year earlier, in 1982, he had married a woman 30 years his junior. The marriage did not last, but custody of the children was awarded to James. Then 10 years later, in May 1993, his ex-wife and her father were returning the children to James after a day out when James drew a gun and proceeded to shoot his ex-father-in-law three times. He then pistol-whipped his ex-wife.

Both victims survived, but James was sentenced to six years in prison. Whilst in prison he suffered a heart attack and underwent triple bypass surgery in the autumn of 1996. He was released in 1997, but died on 21 August after another heart attack.

By then Buster Edwards had been dead almost three years. Since his release in 1975 he had run a flower stall at Waterloo Bridge. In 1987 he'd been incarnated on screen by rock star Phil Collins as a cheeky chappie petty crook in the hit film *Buster*. He and Bruce Reynolds had both been technical advisers on the film, although Reynolds later commented: 'I could barely recognise myself, let alone some other characters.'

On Tuesday 30 November 1994 Edwards's brother found him in a lock-up garage near his flower stall. He had hung himself from a steel girder after a drinking binge. Although darker rumours have circulated, it was assumed he killed himself because of money worries. Bruce Reynolds has suggested he was just bored stiff going straight.

At Edwards's funeral, his wife June's floral tribute spelled out a lyric from 'Two Hearts', which had been the theme tune for the film *Buster*.

Although Bruce Reynolds was given a 25-year sentence, by 1978, nine years into his sentence, he was on day release from prison and soon after out on parole. He and his wife had divorced whilst he was in prison, but they got back together and moved to Streatham. Reynolds was doing odd jobs for old mates. In 1984, however, he was sentenced to three years in prison for supplying amphetamine sulphate. He was out by March 1985.

In 1986 he acted as consultant on *Buster* and in 1995 his autobiography was published. Soon this ex-con had embarked on the literary festival and talk-show circuit. He still lives quietly in Croydon.

Ronnie Biggs was lucky to survive as a free man for so long. He left his address in Melbourne in 1969 virtually as the police were knocking on the door. Early in 1970 he took a liner from Melbourne to Britain via the Panama Canal. He never reached Britain.

According to Anthony Delano's *Slip-Up: How Fleet Street Caught Ronnie Biggs and Scotland Yard Lost Him*, Biggs was virtually broke. Delano claims it had cost him almost £30,000 to get to Australia illegally. He had left £32,000 with various 'bankers' in London, but once he'd gone they'd stolen the lot. He'd paid £10,000 commission to get £40,000 old white fivers changed for new fivers.

His wife, Charmian, left behind in Australia with no money and three children to bring up, sold her story for £65,000 there, with British rights bought by the *Sunday Mirror*.

Biggs meanwhile disembarked at Panama, then travelled to Rio via Caracas, Venezuela. Before he had left Australia he had arranged for a Melbourne solicitor to sell his story, the manuscript authenticated by signature and thumbprint. The

Sun bought it for £20,000.

Ronnie Biggs remained beyond Tommy Butler's reach. It was ironic, therefore, that the report of Butler's early death from cancer, age 57, appeared in the *Sun* newspaper on 21 April 1970, in an edition in which Biggs was telling his story. The *Sun* reported that Butler, an MBE when he died, had been a bachelor who lived with his mother in a small house in Barnes and had no interests outside his work. He'd been twice allowed to postpone his retirement to continue work on the case because, in the newspaper's words, 'he had vowed he would not rest until he got all the robbers behind bars'. The newspaper also noted that, as Reynolds confirmed, Butler was 'always the first to help a crook's family'.

Biggs spent four years in Rio under the name Michael Haynes, working as an odd-jobman, painter and decorator for the expatriate community. By 1984 he was skint. In that year a young journalist from the *Daily Express* got wind of his whereabouts through a friend who'd been in Rio and met Haynes/Biggs.

Biggs was willing to return to England and felt he might be able to do a deal for a reduced sentence, and maybe make some money out of the press interest. What he didn't know but Delano's book makes clear was that the management at the *Express* had told Scotland Yard and Chief Superintendent John Slipper — 'Slipper of the Yard' — was on his way with the journalists to arrest Biggs.

Delano's book describes the ridiculous events that followed. The *Express* got its scoop, but Slipper went home empty-handed. Biggs's girlfriend was pregnant and under Brazilian law no one with a Brazilian dependent can be extradited. (Delano's book was later made into a successful BBC comic drama. Curiously Larry Lamb, the actor who played Biggs in it, had also played Bruce Reynolds in *Buster*.)

Biggs stayed in Brazil, often scuffling for a living by selling T-shirts with his image on them or flogging yet another story to the press. His son Michael, who when unborn had made it possible for Biggs to stay in Brazil, grew up to be a pop star, topping the hit parade by the age of 10. Biggs became his manager. He also became something of a cult character for young British rock bands.

In 1981 bounty hunters kidnapped Biggs and took him to Barbados hoping to sell him to the British authorities. Brazil insisted on his return and finally gave him resident status.

But 20 years later Biggs was in a bad way. He'd suffered three strokes, leaving him partially paralyzed and almost speechless. He wanted to come back to England. According to Reynolds his last wish was 'to walk into a Margate pub as an Englishman and buy a pint of bitter'. He reckoned by now nobody would be interested in the uncompleted part of his sentence. He was wrong.

Again a newspaper brought him home—they even flew Bruce Reynolds out to travel back with him—but the police were waiting on the tarmac when his plane landed and he was immediately whisked away to prison. In August 2007 there were reports in the UK press that he was to be released by February 2008.

THE FORGOTTEN VICTIM —
TRAIN DRIVER JACK MILLS

Perhaps one of the reasons the Great Train Robbery caught the public imagination was because it appeared to be a victimless crime. Nobody could feel sympathy for the banks' loss of money. But whenever a newspaper suggested that the sentences had been too harsh or a Robber's wife sold her story, other newspapers were quick to point out that these train robbers were no heroes and that there was indeed a victim: the driver Jack Mills.

The received view of Mills was that the attack on him shattered his nerves, his health and his life. Further opinion held that this have-a-go hero was treated shamefully by the British Railways Board.

Others have suggested that Mills' health problems were mostly unrelated to the attack, horrific though it was.

A series of memos by the British Railways Board, held at the National Archives, defends the Board's treatment of Mills (AN 171/666). The first, dated 30 October 1969, was inspired by criticism in the press about the way Mills had been treated. This criticism arose from the launch of a Driver Mills Appeal Fund in response to the news that Charmian Biggs was getting £30,000 from the *Sunday Mirror* for her story of life on the run. The appeal raised almost £27,000.

Mills had indeed been off sick a lot since the attack. After the attack, the driver didn't return to work until May 1964. He worked for 18 months on mostly light duties, then was on sick leave suffering from shingles for almost a year from the end of November 1965 to December 1966. In 1967 he was ill for about two and a half months in total before stopping work for good at Christmas.

Sadly, Jack Mills had leukaemia, which eventually killed him. The British Railways Board knew he had leukaemia, but thought that he did not.

> The criticisms [of the way Mills had been treated] are well meant but uninformed and we could only satisfactorily answer them by publicly revealing that Mr Mills is absent not because of the accident but because of an incurable disease which we do not think he knows he has. This is unthinkable and I recommend that we make no reply.

It is said that the British Railways Board refused to facilitate the filming of *Buster* out of respect for Jack Mills. The locomotive involved in the robbery has not been preserved.

UNANSWERED QUESTIONS AND
THE ONES THAT GOT AWAY

There has been no definitive account of who did what during the robbery. The biggest question—who hit Mills—has been discussed in the Introduction. However, it is worth noting that much later Wilfrid Fordham QC, in his attempt to have the long gaol sentences for the robbers reduced, referred to his wife, the journalist Peta Fordham, on the subject.

In a court transcript of the appeal (HO 291/929) the clerk noted:

> She was fully satisfied that the only member of the gang who had used violence, that is to say, the man who struck down the train driver, was Edwards. This was known to all the convicted men, though none of them say so.

Why, then, Reynolds would deny this is not clear unless Fordham was mistaken.

Smaller questions remain unanswered. If we believe Reynolds, Charlie Wilson was the man with the axe who came through the window. (Although Wensley Clarkson in *Killing Charlie* says he was carrying a cosh.) According to Reynolds, the 'assault team' that followed him comprised Jimmy Hussey, Gordon Goody, Bob Welch, Buster Edwards, Tommy Wisbey and two unidentified men.

According to Read, Edwards was the man who earlier had met Whitby, the fireman, on his way back from the disconnected telephone on the track and bundled him down the embankment. The two men waiting there who promised him money have not been identified.

In Read's account Edwards, Jim Hussey and Gordon Goody subdued Mills in his cab and Charlie Wilson wiped the blood from the driver's face with a rag. In this version of events, Gordon Goody aggressively forces Mills to move the train forward to Bridego Bridge.

Neither Reynolds nor Read revealed the identity of the man who later attended to Mills and Whitby on the embankment. In Reynolds's account Biggs remained in one of the Land Rovers. Anthony Delano, however, has Biggs not only telling Mills where to stop the train as he shunted it forward to Bridego Bridge, but also has him down on the embankment cadging a cigarette off Whitby and warning him and Mills about the 'real bastards'. Fordham has Biggs giving the warning and Bob Welch cadging the fag.

Read has an unidentified man warning the postal workers not to move for 30 minutes, while Reynolds doesn't refer to this at all. Fordham implies that it was Gordon Goody.

Reynolds reckoned there were three men who were never caught. One is the train driver—he calls him Peter, but in Read's account he is Stan—who in the event did nothing. The other two he calls 'Frank Munroe' and 'Alf Thomas'. Nobody has ever publicly revealed the identity of these men.

We don't know what became of 'Alf Thomas', but according

to Reynolds 'Frank Munroe' did a bit of film stunt work. He then went into waste paper collection before switching to scrap metal, specializing in recycling steel girders.

There are some Metropolitan Police files in the National Archives that remain closed and it is possible that the identity of at least one of these robbers (the one Hatherill questioned so closely) is revealed in them. It is also possible that we know these men for crimes committed later. But it is also possible that they took their whacks — which, if it was a relatively equal split, would have been around £3 million each in 2008 money — and lived happily ever after. Doubtful though.

Just as nobody has ever shopped these men, so none of the robbers have ever satisfactorily explained who the mysterious man was who told them about the night mail train; why they left their prints all over the farmhouse; who left the bags of money in the woods and why; and who left the money in the phone box and why. Although there have been suspects, Charlie Wilson's murder years after the robbery has never been solved.

The identity of the 'Ulsterman' will probably never be known. The prints in the farmhouse can be explained by catastrophic carelessness. The bags of money found in Dorking Woods and in the phone box are frustratingly intriguing. Was the money in Dorking Woods abandoned in panic? But what was the reason for panic — especially given that these men seemed to be pretty resilient? Was it left to be picked up later? That seems the most likely answer.

The money left in the phone box is actually more mysterious. In 1963 few people had their own phones so public phones were well used. Leaving money in a phone box if it was intended for a particular person (I'm thinking of the 'bung' theory here) would be a very careless way of doing business. The assumption must be that whoever left it there didn't actually care who found it. Perhaps panic, then, was the reason for this.

There were suspects for Charlie Wilson's murder, but their story falls outside the remit of this book. (Clarkson's *Killing Charlie* goes into great detail though still does not have a definitive answer.)

However, the biggest unanswered question remains: what happened to all the money? In the Home Office document about barrister Wilfrid and journalist Peta Fordham previously quoted (HO 291/929), the suggestion from Peta Fordham is that the money had been embezzled by other parties. Certainly, in total only £349,000 was recovered—around a seventh of the £2.6 million haul. Where the rest went, only the surviving robbers know. And, as usual, those who are still alive are not saying.

Sources & Reading

—

There are many files about the Great Train Robbery in the National Archives. They come from the Metropolitan Police, the Buckinghamshire Assizes, the Home Office and the British Railways Board. Much is duplicated.

The accounts of the trials and appeals of the various train robbers are in J 82/420–441 and also ASSI 13/642–764 (and 1029). The Assi (ASSI) files include full lists of exhibits and miscellaneous photographs.

An interesting range of plans, photographs and reports (including the official police report) are gathered alongside information about security arrangements for the robbers whilst in prison in Home Office files: HO 242/1–5; HO 287/1496; HO 391/4 and 242.

Extracting Ronnie Biggs from his Brazilian hidey-hole is discussed in FCO7/2591. British Railways Board discussion papers about driver Jack Mills are in AN 171/666.

There are numerous secondary sources, but all need handling with caution. None are definitive accounts.

Ronnie Biggs, *Ronnie Biggs: His Own Story* (Sphere, 1981)

Wensley Clarkson, *Killing Charlie: The Bloody, Bullet-Riddled Hunt for the Most Powerful Great Train Robber Of All* (Mainstream Publishing, 2006)

Tim Coates, *The Great British Train Robbery, 1963* (Tim Coates, 2003)

Barry Cox, John Shirley and Martin Short, *The Fall of Scotland Yard* (Penguin, 1977)

Anthony Delano, *Slip-Up: How Fleet Street Caught Ronnie Biggs and Scotland Yard Lost Him* (Coronet, 1986)

Peta Fordham, *The Robbers' Tale* (Hodder & Stoughton, 1965)

Freddie Foreman, *Brown Bread Fred: The Autobiography of the Godfather of British Crime* (John Blake, 2007)

Frank Fraser and James Morton, *Mad Frank* and *Mad Frank and Friends Omnibus* (Time Warner, 2003)

George Hatherill, *A Detective's Story* (McGraw-Hill, US, 1971)

Piers Paul Read, *The Train Robbers* (W.H. Allen, 1978)

Bruce Reynolds, *The Autobiography of a Thief* (Virgin, 2005)

AUTHOR'S ACKNOWLEDGEMENTS

Above all my thanks go to Sheila Knight — a great editor — but also to Catherine Bradley and Slaney Begley.

PICTURE ACKNOWLEDGEMENTS

Most pictures can be seen at The National Archives and are © Crown copyright unless otherwise stated here. **1, 2, 3, 4, 5, 6, 7, 10, 11, 13, 14, 16** © Thames Valley Police. By kind permission of the Curator of Thames Valley Police Museum Sulhamstead. **8, 9, 19, 20** © Metropolitan Police. **12** and **18** are supplied by Mirrorpix.

Index

—